21 Secrets to Success, Greatness, Happiness, and Richness

By

FAROOKH SENSEI

For permission requests, please get in touch with the author directly at:

Farookh Sensei
team@farookhsensei.com
www.farookhsensei.com

Disclaimer

This book draws from the author's personal experiences and research, aiming to provide educational and informational content. The author and publisher do not guarantee the accuracy or completeness of the information presented. The advice and strategies offered may not be suitable for every situation, and the author is not responsible for any loss or damage resulting from using this book.

Trademarks

First Edition: **December 2024**

Printed in **India**

Thanks

Thanks to Dr Rithin Ismail, Mamta Joshi, Febin P, Nisha Muthalib, and Ami Rashid for proofreading this book.

Dedication

I dedicate this book to everyone who seeks to redefine success, greatness, happiness, and richness on their terms and commits to continuous growth and self-improvement. May your journey be filled with learning, achievement, and fulfilment.

Table Of Contents

Discovering a New Path to Success, Greatness, Happiness, and Richness

In a world where success is often measured by wealth and power, it's easy to lose sight of what truly matters. This book invites you to embark on a personal journey to redefine success, greatness, happiness, and richness in a way that resonates with your heart and soul. Rather than following society's one-size-fits-all formula, you'll explore a path that aligns with your unique values and dreams.

Have you ever felt that conventional definitions of success don't resonate with who you indeed are? The relentless pursuit of money and status has left you feeling unfulfilled. You're not alone. Many people feel trapped by societal expectations, chasing goals that don't bring genuine satisfaction. This book challenges those traditional notions and encourages you to envision a version of success that brings true joy and fulfilment.

Imagine waking up daily with purpose, knowing that your actions reflect your deepest values. Envision a life where success is not just about external achievements but personal growth, meaningful relationships, and contributing to something greater than yourself. Together, we'll explore how to make this vision a reality.

Who Is This Book For?

This book is for anyone eager to redefine success on their own terms. Whether you're a leader, entrepreneur, professional seeking more meaning in your work, or someone at a crossroads, the insights within these pages are designed to guide you toward a more fulfilling path. If you're eager to break free from societal pressures and live authentically, this book offers the tools and perspectives to help you get there.

Your Journey Begins Here

As you delve into the "21 Secrets to Success, Greatness, Happiness, and Richness," reflect on your definitions of these concepts. Consider what truly brings you joy and fulfilment. Are the goals you're pursuing your own, or are they inherited from societal expectations? This journey is about embracing authenticity, fostering personal growth, and having the courage to live on your terms.

Farookh Sensei

Leadership MasterCoach
LEDGE International

What is Success?

Success Equals Freedom

For some, success means achieving true freedom in life. Success isn't just about external milestones like wealth or status but about the ability to live in alignment with one's values, passions, and desires. This freedom allows them to make choices based on what truly matters to them without being constrained by societal pressures or expectations. Whether it's financial independence, control over their time, or the ability to pursue their passions, true success for these individuals is the freedom to live on their terms.

Financial Freedom: Financial freedom allows you to live without constant worry about money, supporting your desired lifestyle while focusing on what truly matters to you, such as passion projects and personal fulfilment.

Time Freedom: Time freedom gives you control over your schedule, allowing you to spend time on activities that bring joy and fulfilment rather than feeling obligated to follow rigid, externally imposed structures.

Location Freedom: Location freedom allows you to live and work wherever you choose, embracing new environments, cultures, and experiences without being tied to a specific place.

Choice Freedom: Choice freedom empowers you to make decisions based on your values and desires, freeing you from fear, obligation, or societal pressure. It enables you to design a life that aligns with your true self.

Purpose Freedom: Purpose freedom means living a life aligned with your mission and passions, giving you a sense of direction and meaning, where a higher purpose drives your work and actions, not just external rewards.

Success Equals Passion

For some people, success equals following their passion. It's not about wealth, status, or traditional achievements but about aligning their work with what they love. When passion drives their efforts, work transforms into a fulfilling pursuit rather than a mere obligation. Challenges are not roadblocks but stepping stones for these individuals, fuelling their perseverance and creativity. Success, for them, is defined by the joy and satisfaction that comes from doing what they are passionate about, making each accomplishment feel more meaningful and personal.

Success Equals Positive Impact

For some, success is about making a positive impact on others. It goes beyond personal achievements or material gain, focusing on contributing to the well-being of those around them. Acts of kindness, mentorship, or more significant initiatives provide a more profound sense of purpose that material success alone cannot offer. True fulfilment comes from knowing that actions have made a meaningful difference in the lives of others, creating a ripple effect that enhances both personal satisfaction and the world at large.

Success Equals Health and Well-being

For some, success is deeply connected to health and well-being. Physical and mental wellness provide the foundation for pursuing passions, helping others, and thoroughly enjoying life's experiences. When self-care—through nutrition, exercise, mindfulness, and rest—is prioritised, it creates the energy and vitality needed to engage meaningfully with the world. Achieving and maintaining good health enables one to pursue goals with clarity and strength, making well-being an essential element of success.

Success Equals Purposeful Living

For some, success is about discovering and living their purpose. A clear sense of purpose is a compass, guiding decisions and actions with intention and meaning. It helps focus energy on what truly matters, offering direction and fulfilment. Aligning life with purpose ensures that each step resonates with core values and aspirations, creating a more profound sense of satisfaction and accomplishment. Living with purpose transforms success into a journey of authenticity and personal growth.

Success Equals Meaningful Relationships

For some, success is found in cultivating meaningful relationships. True fulfilment comes from deep connections through love, friendships, or family ties. These relationships enrich life in profound ways, offering joy, support, and shared experiences that make life more vibrant. Success, in this view, is not only about individual accomplishments but also about the quality of the bonds we form and the lasting impact they have on our happiness and well-being.

Success Equals Inner Peace

For some, success is about achieving inner peace. This mental and emotionally calm state allows one to remain centred, even amid life's stressors. Cultivating inner peace through mindfulness, gratitude, and releasing negativity enhances the ability to navigate challenges with grace and resilience. It provides a sense of fulfilment and contentment, making inner peace vital to true happiness and lasting success.

Success Equals Personal Growth

For some, success is about embracing change and personal growth. As life evolves, so do the definitions of success, greatness, happiness, and richness. New experiences and insights shift what brings fulfilment. By accepting this fluidity, individuals can adapt their goals and aspirations, ensuring they stay true to their authentic selves while continuously growing and evolving.

Success Equals Happiness

For some, success equals happiness. Cultivating gratitude shifts attention from what's missing to what's already present, enhancing overall well-being. This practice fosters a positive mindset, allowing you to appreciate life's blessings and attract greater fulfilment. Regularly acknowledging the good in your life creates a foundation for lasting happiness and inner contentment.

Success Equals Finding Balance in Life

For some, success equals finding balance in life. Striking harmony between career, relationships, personal growth, and leisure is crucial for well-being. This balance helps prevent burnout and ensures time and energy are dedicated to what truly matters. Achieving it requires setting priorities, establishing boundaries, and practising self-discipline, leading to a more fulfilling and sustainable life.

Success Equals Lasting Legacy

For some, success is about leaving a lasting legacy. It's not always about grand achievements but the values imparted to others, the positive influence on colleagues, or contributions to the community. This mindset shapes actions today, giving depth and meaning to life's pursuits. A legacy reflects the lasting impact one leaves on the world, ensuring that success transcends personal accomplishments and creates enduring value for others.

1.

21 Myths About Success

These myths focus on **external markers of success**, personal behaviour, societal expectations, and misconceptions about what it means to achieve success. They are separate from greatness (which focuses on personal traits and legacy) and richness (which deals with financisal aspects).

Myth 1: Success is All About Luck

Explanation: Many believe success is about being in the right place and time. While luck can play a role, it's not the main factor.

Why This Myth Misleads: Relying on luck alone undermines the power of hard work and preparation. Luck may provide an opportunity, but without readiness, it's wasted. This myth leads people to wait passively for success rather than taking control of their own actions.

The Truth: Success is about making your own luck through consistent effort and preparing for opportunities. By working hard and staying proactive, you create the circumstances where luck can benefit you. True success combines preparation with seizing the right moment.

Example: A job applicant may stumble upon a great opportunity, but without the right qualifications or skills, they won't be able to capitalise on it.

Myth 2: Success is All About Constant Action and Being Busy

Explanation: There's a belief that the more you do, the more successful you'll be. Staying busy is often mistaken for progress.

Why This Myth Misleads: Constant busyness can lead to burnout and poor health without achieving progress. It promotes the idea that activity is more important than effectiveness. Focusing on quantity over quality leads to saving energy on unimportant tasks.

The Truth: Success requires focused, intentional effort. Strategic rest and reflection are just as important as action. By prioritising high-impact tasks, you make meaningful progress rather than just staying busy.

Example: A CEO who schedules back-to-back meetings all day may seem productive but fails to focus on critical decisions that drive the company's growth.

Myth 3: Success is About Doing It All

Explanation: Some people think success requires handling every task independently. This belief glorifies self-sufficiency and discourages collaboration.

Why This Myth Misleads: Attempting to do everything yourself leads to exhaustion and inefficiency. It prevents you from leveraging other people's strengths, which can elevate your own success. This mindset reduces your ability to focus on what truly matters.

The Truth: Success comes from effective delegation and focusing on your strengths. By sharing tasks, you free up time for high-value activities. Collaboration creates more opportunities for growth and innovation.

Example: An entrepreneur attempting to manage marketing, operations, and finance alone will likely fall short in at least one area, limiting the business's overall success.

Myth 4: Success Requires a Ruthless, Competitive Mindset

Explanation: Many think success demands a cutthroat attitude and that one should see others as rivals. This belief promotes a win-at-all-costs mentality.

Why This Myth Misleads: Ruthlessness breeds distrust, damaging relationships that could lead to long-term opportunities. It creates an atmosphere of insecurity where collaboration is overlooked. Over time, this competitive mindset harms more than it helps.

The Truth: Success thrives on empathy, collaboration, and ethical behaviour. Working with others creates shared success and builds lasting trust. Helping others succeed often results in mutual growth and better opportunities.

Example: A manager who hoards resources and knowledge to outdo colleagues will eventually lose the team's respect and cooperation, limiting overall success.

Myth 5: Success Requires Following a Strict Formula or Set of Rules

Explanation: Some believe success comes from following a proven path or sticking to a rigid formula. This mindset discourages creative thinking.

Why This Myth Misleads: Rigidly following rules limits innovation and adaptability. Every individual and situation is unique, and what works for one person may not work for another. This belief promotes conformity, which often stifles personal growth.

The Truth: Success comes from finding your own path and being flexible enough to adapt. Creative problem-solving and risk-taking lead to breakthroughs. Each person's journey is different, so success requires personal discovery and innovation.

Example: A business that sticks to outdated industry norms without adapting to new technology will fall behind competitors who innovate.

Myth 6: Success Means Having Everything Figured Out

Explanation: Many think that to be successful, you must always have a clear plan and know exactly what to do. This myth creates unnecessary pressure.

Why This Myth Misleads: Success is rarely linear, and even the most successful people need more certainty. Expecting to have everything figured out leads to overthinking and hesitation. The pursuit of certainty can slow down progress and prevent action.

The Truth: Success is about learning and adapting as you go. It's okay not to have all the answers from the start. Flexibility and resilience in the face of uncertainty lead to growth and progress.

Example: A startup founder who embraces change and learns from mistakes will often find greater success than someone who waits for the perfect plan.

Myth 7: The More Talents You Have, The More Successful You'll Be

Explanation: Some think success comes from mastering many different skills at once. This belief can lead to being a jack-of-all-trades master of none.

Why This Myth Misleads: Spreading yourself too thin dilutes focus and prevents deep mastery in any area. It promotes the idea that breadth is more important than depth. Without specialisation, it's harder to stand out and create lasting value.

The Truth: Success often comes from focusing on one core skill and becoming exceptional. Mastery and expertise in one field typically have a more significant impact than having shallow knowledge in many areas.

Example: A professional athlete excels by focusing on perfecting one sport rather than attempting to be average at multiple sports.

Myth 8: You Must Be a Perfectionist to Succeed

Explanation: Perfectionism is often seen as the key to success, with people believing everything must be flawless. This myth causes unnecessary stress.

Why This Myth Misleads: Perfectionism leads to procrastination, burnout, and missed opportunities. It slows progress because you become obsessed with getting everything right rather than moving forward. Perfection also doesn't guarantee success—often, it just delays it.

The Truth: Success comes from progress, not perfection. Embracing imperfection allows you to learn from mistakes and adapt. Taking action, even if imperfect, moves you closer to your goals.

Example: A product designer who waits for a perfect launch may miss the market window. At the same time, one who releases an early version and iterates finds faster success.

Myth 9: Success Means Having a Perfect Plan

Explanation: Many believe you need a flawless, detailed plan for success. This myth overemphasises planning over action.

Why This Myth Misleads: Over-planning creates rigidity and prevents flexibility in the face of change. Circumstances often evolve, and sticking to a "perfect" plan can leave you stuck when you need to adapt. The real world rarely unfolds according to plan.

The Truth: Success favours adaptable and flexible people. While a plan provides direction, being open to change and ready to pivot ensures progress. Adjusting as you go often leads to more success than a rigid plan.

Example: A company that adapts its business strategy in response to market changes will succeed over one that sticks stubbornly to a failing plan.

Myth 10: You Have to Sacrifice Happiness, Sleep, and Relationships to Be Successful

Explanation: Some believe success requires sacrificing personal joy, rest, and relationships. This myth promotes an unbalanced, unhealthy approach.

Why This Myth Misleads: Neglecting personal happiness and relationships leads to burnout and dissatisfaction. Short-term gains achieved through sacrifice are often unsustainable in the long run. Success without well-being and meaningful connections is hollow.

The Truth: Success and happiness can coexist. Maintaining a balance between work and personal life leads to sustained success and fulfilment. Solid relationships and well-being enhance one's ability to perform at best.

Example: A business leader who invests in personal time and family relationships stays energised and more effective over the long term.

Myth 11: Success Requires Sacrificing Integrity

Explanation: Some believe cutting corners and compromising values is the only way to get ahead. This myth suggests that ethics and success are incompatible.

Why This Myth Misleads: Short-term gains achieved through unethical behaviour rarely last and often lead to long-term damage; losing trust and credibility harms future opportunities. Integrity is a cornerstone of lasting success, not a barrier to it.

The Truth: True success is built on trust, honesty, and ethics. Maintaining your integrity leads to more meaningful success and strengthens relationships and reputation. Ethical decisions create sustainable growth.

Example: A company prioritising fair treatment of employees and customers may grow slower but build a loyal customer base that drives long-term success.

Myth 12: Success is Only About Money

Explanation: Many believe that financial wealth is the only marker of success. This myth reduces success to a single metric.

Why This Myth Misleads: Money alone cannot bring fulfilment or happiness. Focusing solely on financial success can lead to a lack of balance and neglect of personal growth, relationships, or impact. True success is multifaceted and goes beyond financial gain.

The Truth: Success is about holistic growth, which includes financial stability, personal fulfilment, strong relationships, and meaningful contributions. A balanced life where personal and financial goals align leads to lasting success.

Example: A millionaire who feels disconnected from family and needs a sense of purpose may feel more successful despite their financial wealth.

Myth 13: Success Requires a High-Risk Personality

Explanation: Some believe success only comes to those willing to take significant risks. This myth glorifies high-stakes gambles as a path to success.

Why This Myth Misleads: Reckless risk-taking can lead to failure more often than success. High-risk decisions without proper preparation or research usually result in unnecessary losses. Success isn't about luck or chance but about informed, calculated risks.

The Truth: Balanced risk-taking, where you carefully evaluate pros and cons, leads to sustainable success. Successful people take risks but do so with caution and a clear understanding of potential outcomes. Smart risks create opportunities while minimising unnecessary losses.

Example: A successful investor doesn't bet on risky stocks without research but makes informed decisions after analyzing the market.

Myth 14: Success is Always Visible

Explanation: Many believe success must be seen and validated by others. This myth ties success to public recognition and external approval.

Why This Myth Misleads: Internal and personal successes are often invisible to the outside world but just as important. Defining success based on visibility can lead to a superficial pursuit of recognition rather than meaningful fulfilment. True success isn't always on display.

The Truth: Success is personal and doesn't always need external validation. Private victories, personal growth, and fulfilment are equally important measures of success. Quiet, internal achievements often lead to more profound satisfaction than public recognition.

Example: An artist who finds personal fulfilment through their work, even without widespread fame, is successful by their standards.

Myth 15: Success Means Meeting Society's Expectations

Explanation: There's a belief that societal norms and expectations define success. This myth suggests that you must fit into a predefined mould.

Why This Myth Misleads: Society's definition of success often ignores individuality and personal goals. Chasing societal approval can lead to unfulfilling achievements that don't align with your values. It limits success to a one-size-fits-all standard that may not resonate with everyone.

The Truth: True success is personal and unique, defined by your values and goals, not external pressures. Fulfilment comes from pursuing what matters to you, even if it doesn't match society's ideals. The most meaningful success is deeply personal and self-defined.

Example: A person who chooses a modest, purpose-driven career over a high-status job may feel more successful.

Myth 16: Success is Easy for Those Who Have Connections

Explanation: There's a belief that having connections guarantees an easy path to success. This myth diminishes the value of hard work and effort.

Why This Myth Misleads: Connections may open doors but don't guarantee success. People must still prove themselves, deliver results, and build on opportunities. Without effort and value, connections alone won't sustain long-term success.

The Truth: Success comes from skill, perseverance, and delivering results, even if connections help get you started. Hard work, integrity, and effort are essential to capitalise on opportunities. Long-term success is earned through competence, not just relationships.

Example: An employee who lands a job through a referral but fails to perform will likely lose the position, regardless of their connections.

Myth 17: You Need a Lot of Resources to Be Successful

Explanation: Many believe success requires abundant resources, such as money, education, or networks. This myth makes success seem inaccessible to many.

Why This Myth Misleads: While resources help, they aren't the only path to success; despite limited resource access, many succeed through creativity, resilience, and resourcefulness. This myth discourages those with less, making them think success is out of reach.

The Truth: Resourcefulness, innovation, and resilience are more critical to success than having abundant resources. Success is about making the most of what you have and finding creative solutions to overcome obstacles. Many successful people started with little but achieved great things through perseverance.

Example: A self-taught entrepreneur who builds a successful business from scratch with minimal investment exemplifies resourcefulness over wealth.

Myth 18: Success Requires Always Being Serious

Explanation: Many believe that seriousness and intensity are required for success. This myth promotes the idea that light-heartedness and fun hinder progress.

Why This Myth Misleads: A rigid, all-serious approach can stifle creativity, limit problem-solving, and lead to burnout. It creates an unhealthy work environment and reduces the ability to enjoy the journey. Success is not about constant seriousness but balance.

The Truth: Success thrives on balance, humour, and flexibility. Light-hearted moments foster creativity and relieve stress, leading to better performance. Embracing joy and humour allows for a more enjoyable and sustainable journey to success.

Example: A workplace that fosters collaboration and humour while maintaining focus often sees higher productivity and innovation than one that prioritizes intensity alone.

Myth 19: Success is a Destination

Explanation: There's a belief that success is the final point you reach, after which you stop striving. This myth treats success as a fixed state.

Why This Myth Misleads: Success is not static, and treating it as a final destination limits further growth. Once a goal is achieved, new challenges and opportunities arise. Stopping once success is reached often leads to stagnation.

The Truth: Success is a journey of continuous growth, learning, and adaptation. Each success opens the door to new opportunities for improvement. The most successful people keep evolving, knowing success requires ongoing effort and reinvention.

Example: An athlete who wins a championship but stops training will likely fall behind, while one who continues improving will sustain success.

Myth 20: Success Means Never Saying No to Opportunities

Explanation: Many believe that saying "yes" to every opportunity is key to success. This myth encourages overcommitment and lack of focus.

Why This Myth Misleads: Saying yes to everything dilutes focus and leads to burnout; not all opportunities align with your goals, and accepting too many can prevent you from excelling in the areas that matter most. Spreading yourself too thin harms long-term success.

The Truth: Success comes from knowing when to say "no" to protect your time and energy. Being selective about opportunities lets you focus on what drives results and progress. Strategic focus, rather than over-commitment, leads to lasting success.

Example: A business leader who rejects low-value partnerships can focus on strategic initiatives that drive significant growth.

Myth 21: Success Means Never Asking for Help

Explanation: Many believe that successful people achieve everything on their own. This myth glorifies independence over collaboration.

Why This Myth Misleads: No one succeeds in isolation. Attempting to do everything alone limits your growth and prevents learning from others. Collaboration accelerates success by leveraging the expertise and support of others.

The Truth: Success is often a team effort, and knowing when to ask for help is a strength, not a weakness. Seeking mentorship, collaboration, and support opens new opportunities and faster growth. Success is built on shared efforts.

Example: A startup founder who seeks guidance from mentors and experts builds a stronger business faster than one who insists on learning everything alone.

2.

21 Myths about Greatness

These myths concentrate on **personal development, leadership, influence**, and the false notions of what makes someone "great." They do not overlap with success or richness; they emphasise impact, legacy, and personal values over accomplishments and material wealth.

Myth 1: Greatness is Achieved Quickly

Explanation: Many believe that greatness happens overnight without long-term effort. They think that once you start something, success should follow rapidly.

Why This Myth Misleads: True greatness results from years of hard work, learning, and growth; instant success is often unsustainable because it lacks the foundation built through experience. Expecting quick results can lead to disappointment and giving up too early.

The Truth: Greatness takes time, dedication, and continuous effort over an extended period. It is cultivated through persistence, discipline, and constant learning. The slow journey toward greatness builds resilience and true mastery.

Example: An entrepreneur who expects immediate success after launching a business may become frustrated, while someone who perseveres through challenges eventually achieves long-lasting greatness.

Myth 2: Greatness Requires External Validation

Explanation: Some believe that greatness is only achieved when others acknowledge and praise it. This myth suggests that public recognition is essential for true greatness.

Why This Myth Misleads: Greatness doesn't rely on external validation. Many who contribute significantly do so quietly, without the limelight or public applause. Seeking validation can distract from the meaningful work required to achieve greatness.

The Truth: Greatness is about the impact and value you create, regardless of whether others recognise it. True greatness is internal, fuelled by purpose and commitment, not the need for approval. People often achieve greatness without ever being in the public eye.

Example: A doctor who saves lives daily without recognition still achieves greatness, proving that validation from others isn't necessary to be great.

Myth 3: Greatness Means Being Better Than Others

Explanation: Many think greatness is about outshining or defeating others in competition. They believe comparison is the key to measuring greatness.

Why This Myth Misleads: Constant comparison to others often leads to insecurity and unhealthy competition. True greatness is not about beating others but mastering yourself and your craft. Focusing on others takes your attention away from your personal growth.

The Truth: Greatness is about personal achievement, self-mastery, and becoming your best version, not outdoing others. Your true competition is with who you were yesterday, not with others. Internal goals and values drive true greatness.

Example: An athlete who sets personal records and improves daily is achieving greatness, even if they aren't always the competition winner.

Myth 4: Greatness Comes from Birth

Explanation: There's a belief that people are born great and that it's a natural gift, not something earned. Some think greatness is an innate quality that can't be developed.

Why This Myth Misleads: Greatness isn't something you're born with; it's something you build through hard work and learning. Many people who achieve greatness do so through perseverance, not natural-born talent. Believing greatness is innate limits personal effort and growth.

The Truth: Anyone can achieve greatness by developing the right habits, mindset, and skills. Greatness is built through effort, dedication, and continuous learning. It results from what you do, not what you're born with.

Example: An artist with no formal training who rises to greatness through years of practice demonstrates that greatness is not something you are born with.

Myth 5: You Need to Be Famous to Be Great

Explanation: Some people believe that greatness and fame go hand in hand. They think you can't be considered great if people don't know your name.

Why This Myth Misleads: Fame is often mistaken for greatness, but they are different. Public recognition does not equate to genuine impact or lasting contributions. Fame can be fleeting, while greatness is based on substance and the lasting difference you make.

The Truth: Greatness is about the positive impact you create, not the fame you achieve. Many people work behind the scenes and quietly create lasting change without being famous. True greatness is built on the lives you touch, not the attention you receive.

Example: A humanitarian who makes a profound difference in a small community, without media coverage or fame, still exemplifies greatness.

Myth 6: Greatness is Limited to Certain Fields

Explanation: Some believe that greatness can only be achieved in high-profile fields such as sports, entertainment, or business. They assume that only these professions offer the potential for true greatness.

Why This Myth Misleads: Greatness is not confined to a few well-known fields. People excel in various professions, including education, healthcare, science, and community service. Limiting greatness to specific industries diminishes the value of contributions made in less publicised fields.

The Truth: Greatness can be found in any field where meaningful contributions are made. Whether in teaching, social work, or local leadership, greatness is defined by your positive impact on others and your commitment to excellence. Every field offers opportunities for greatness through innovation, dedication, and purpose.

Example: A nurse who provides compassionate care and improves patients' lives daily achieves greatness in healthcare, proving that greatness isn't limited to prestigious or well-known professions.

Myth 7: Only Extroverts Can Be Great

Explanation: Many believe greatness requires being outgoing, highly social, and visible. They think introverts lack the personality traits needed to achieve greatness.

Why This Myth Misleads: Greatness is not tied to extroversion or being in the public eye. Many introverts achieve greatness through focus, creativity, and deep thinking. Overvaluing extroversion overlooks the unique strengths that introverts bring to leadership and achievement.

The Truth: Both introverts and extroverts can achieve greatness in different ways, using their strengths. Introverts excel in fields requiring deep thought and focus, while extroverts may thrive in social or public roles. Greatness is defined by actions and impact, not personality type.

Example: A reserved scientist who makes groundbreaking discoveries proves that introverts can achieve greatness without being socially dominant.

Myth 8: Greatness Requires Constant Hustle

Explanation: There's a belief that greatness comes only from nonstop work and constant activity. People believe that taking breaks or resting slows down the path to greatness.

Why This Myth Misleads: Constant hustle often leads to burnout, not greatness. Overworking can diminish long-term progress, while rest and reflection enhance creativity and focus. The idea that greatness requires endless work overlooks the importance of balance.

The Truth: Greatness comes from focused, strategic effort and maintaining a healthy balance between work and rest. Rest is essential for long-term success and avoiding burnout. Sustainable greatness is built on smart, intentional work, not exhaustion.

Example: A business owner who takes time to rest and reflect achieves sustainable success, while someone who constantly works without pause risks burnout and failure.

Myth 9: Greatness is Determined by Talent Alone

Explanation: Many believe that greatness is only achievable by those with natural talent. They think that without talent, you can't reach the top.

Why This Myth Misleads: Talent alone doesn't guarantee greatness. It requires discipline, hard work, and continuous learning to develop talent into greatness fully. Those who rely only on talent without effort often fall short of their potential.

The Truth: Greatness is shaped more by effort, persistence, and growth than raw talent. Many people with moderate talent achieve greatness by dedicating themselves to learning and improving. Hard work and resilience often surpass talent in achieving long-term greatness.

Example: A musician with modest initial skills who practices daily and refines their craft achieves greatness through effort rather than relying solely on natural talent.

Myth 10: Greatness Requires Sacrificing Everything

Explanation: Some think achieving greatness means giving up everything else, including relationships, health, and personal happiness. They believe that greatness demands complete and total sacrifice.

Why This Myth Misleads: Sacrificing everything for greatness often leads to burnout, isolation, and dissatisfaction. True greatness does not require destroying other aspects of your life; balance is essential for lasting success. Support systems and personal well-being contribute to achieving and sustaining greatness.

The Truth: You can achieve greatness without sacrificing your happiness, relationships, or health. Greatness is more sustainable and meaningful when shared with loved ones and balanced with personal fulfilment. A healthy, happy life often fuels greater accomplishments.

Example: An athlete who maintains strong family connections and practices self-care while excelling in their sport demonstrates that greatness and balance coexist.

Myth 11: Greatness is Easy For those Who Have It

Explanation: There's a belief that if someone is destined for greatness, it will come quickly to them. This myth suggests that greatness is a smooth journey for those who are meant to be great.

Why This Myth Misleads: Even the most outstanding individuals face setbacks, challenges, and failures. The path to greatness is filled with obstacles that test resilience and perseverance. Believing that greatness should be easy discourages those who struggle, making them think they can't achieve it.

The Truth: Greatness requires overcoming adversity, learning from mistakes, and continuously pushing through difficulties. Those who face the most complex challenges often rise to the most incredible heights. The journey to greatness is rarely smooth but builds strength and character.

Example: A successful entrepreneur who failed multiple times before building a thriving business shows that greatness comes from persistence, not ease.

Myth 12: Greatness Means Never Failing

Explanation: Some believe that greatness is about avoiding failure altogether. They think that great people don't experience setbacks or mistakes.

Why This Myth Misleads: Failure is an integral part of the journey toward greatness. It provides valuable lessons and fosters personal growth. Viewing failure as a negative or a sign of inadequacy prevents people from reaching their full potential.

The Truth: Greatness often emerges from the lessons learned through failure. Failure is a stepping stone to greater success, offering insights that help you improve and grow. Those who embrace failure as part of their journey often achieve greater heights.

Example: An inventor who learns from multiple failed prototypes eventually creates a groundbreaking innovation, proving that failure is part of achieving greatness.

Myth 13: Greatness Means Always Being in Control

Explanation: Some believe that being excellent means controlling every situation and never letting go of power. They think that greatness comes from micromanaging and never delegating.

Why This Myth Misleads: Constant control can stifle creativity and disempower others. True greatness involves knowing when to let go and trusting others to contribute. Great leaders understand that holding on to everything limits progress and creativity.

The Truth: Great leaders empower others by delegating and trusting their team, knowing when to relinquish control and allowing others to lead, fostering growth and innovation. True greatness is collaborative, not controlling.

Example: A project manager who delegates key tasks to their team and supports their ideas demonstrates that greatness comes from empowering others, not controlling every detail.

Myth 14: Greatness is a Gift Only for the Young

Explanation: Many believe that greatness can only be achieved in youth, and if you haven't reached it early, your chance is gone. They think that only young people can make a significant impact.

Why This Myth Misleads: Greatness can be achieved at any age, and experience often enhances one's ability to make meaningful contributions. Many people reach their peak and accomplish their most extraordinary feats later in life. Limiting greatness to youth ignores the potential for wisdom and maturity to drive greatness.

The Truth: Greatness is not confined to youth—people achieve greatness at all stages of life. Experience and perspective often fuel the most significant achievements later in life. It's never too late to pursue greatness, regardless of your age.

Example: A retired professional who starts a new business or non-profit in their later years demonstrates that greatness can be achieved anywhere in life.

Myth 15: Greatness Requires Extraordinary Intelligence

Explanation: Some believe that only knowledgeable people can achieve greatness. They think that you need to be a genius to reach the top.

Why This Myth Misleads: Intelligence alone doesn't guarantee greatness. Emotional intelligence, creativity, and perseverance often play a more significant role than IQ. Many people with average intelligence achieve greatness through hard work and determination.

The Truth: Greatness is built more on effort, creativity, and resilience than raw intelligence. Emotional intelligence and the ability to adapt often matter more than IQ. Regardless of intellectual ability, anyone can achieve greatness through dedication and hard work.

Example: A community leader with average academic performance who builds a successful initiative through passion and persistence shows that greatness is about more than just intelligence.

Myth 16: Greatness Means Never Changing Your Mind

Explanation: There's a belief that great people never change their minds or opinions and stick firmly to their initial decisions. Some think that changing your mind shows weakness.

Why This Myth Misleads: Stubbornness can limit growth and prevent innovation. Great individuals are adaptable and open to new information, allowing them to evolve and make better decisions. Refusing to change your mind can close off new opportunities and hinder greatness.

The Truth: Greatness involves learning, adapting, and knowing when to change direction for the better. Flexibility is key to long-term success and relevance. Great leaders will admit mistakes and adjust their course for more significant outcomes.

Example: A CEO who changes their company's strategy based on new market trends shows that greatness involves being adaptable, not rigid.

Myth 17: Greatness is Reserved for Certain Professions

Explanation: Some people think that only those in high-profile professions, such as politics or business, can achieve greatness. They believe that greatness is tied to specific roles or fields.

Why This Myth Misleads: Greatness can be found in every profession and field. Whether teaching, healthcare, or local community service, people achieve greatness by making meaningful contributions in their areas of expertise. Limiting greatness to certain professions diminishes the value of other vital roles.

The Truth: Greatness is about the impact and value you bring, regardless of your job or profession. Every profession offers the potential for greatness through dedication, passion, and purpose. True greatness can be achieved by anyone who strives to make a difference in their field.

Example: A schoolteacher who inspires countless students and shapes their futures achieves greatness through education, proving that greatness is not confined to high-status jobs.

Myth 18: Greatness is Static

Explanation: Some people believe that once greatness is achieved, it's permanent and doesn't need to be maintained. They think that once you're great, you'll always be great.

Why This Myth Misleads: Greatness requires continuous growth and effort to maintain. Complacency can erode greatness over time, as resting on past achievements without further development can cause decline. Achieving greatness once doesn't guarantee it will last without ongoing improvement.

The Truth: Greatness is dynamic and must be nurtured through continuous learning, growth, and adaptation. It's about staying relevant, evolving, and striving to improve consistently. Maintaining greatness requires the same effort and dedication as achieving it initially.

Example: A highly successful athlete who continues to train and improve after reaching the top of their field demonstrates that greatness requires ongoing effort to sustain.

Myth 19: Greatness Must Be Recognized by the Masses

Explanation: Some believe that greatness requires widespread recognition and that you can't be great unless your achievements are known by many. This myth assumes that the more people know about you, the greater you are.

Why This Myth Misleads: Public recognition is not necessary for greatness. Many people make significant contributions and achieve greatness without being widely known or celebrated. Seeking external recognition can also distract from meaningful work and impact.

The Truth: Greatness doesn't need to be validated by the masses. It's about the value you create and your impact, even if only a few people notice. True greatness is often quiet, personal, and focused on making a difference in specific areas or communities.

Example: A volunteer who dedicates their life to improving a small community without media attention proves that greatness doesn't require widespread recognition.

Myth 20: Greatness Comes from Winning

Explanation: Many believe greatness is about winning and being the best at everything. They think that to be great, you must always come out on top and never lose.

Why This Myth Misleads: Focusing only on winning can lead to compromising values or ignoring the lessons from losing. Greatness is not about always winning; it's about how you face challenges, how you grow, and what you stand for. Winning at all costs can sometimes diminish greatness.

The Truth: Greatness comes from approaching challenges and handling victories and defeats with grace, integrity, and resilience. It's about your character and the lessons learned, not just the outcome of every competition. People can achieve greatness through their values, even in defeat.

Example: An athlete who loses a crucial match but inspires others through their sportsmanship and perseverance demonstrates that greatness is not just about winning.

Myth 21: Greatness Means Always Being Right

Explanation: Some believe greatness means never making mistakes and always having the correct answer. They think that great people are infallible and never admit to being wrong.

Why This Myth Misleads: No one is always right, and believing so limits growth, learning, and self-improvement. Greatness comes from admitting mistakes, learning from them, and remaining open to new ideas and perspectives. Insisting on always being right can block progress and stifle innovation.

The Truth: Great individuals are willing to admit when they're wrong and embrace opportunities to learn and grow. Greatness is built on humility, openness, and a mindset of continuous improvement. Those who are great are learners first, not those who insist on always being right.

Example: A business leader who changes their approach after realising a mistake strengthens their greatness by showing adaptability and growth, proving that greatness includes learning from failure.

3.

21 Myths about Happiness

These myths focus on **internal and emotional states**, misconceptions about relationships, and external circumstances tied to happiness.

Myth 1: Happiness is Constant

Explanation: Many believe that once you achieve happiness, it will stay with you constantly. This myth suggests that true happiness means always being in a positive state.

Why This Myth Misleads: Happiness fluctuates with life's ups and downs. Expecting it to be constant creates pressure to always feel good, which is unrealistic. This belief can lead to disappointment when natural emotions like sadness or frustration arise.

The Truth: Happiness comes and goes, much like other emotions. It's about finding joy in moments, not sustaining it constantly. True happiness is about appreciating good times and learning from challenges.

Example: A person who experiences periods of stress at work but finds joy with friends on the weekends understands that happiness isn't constant but is found in moments.

Myth 2: Money Buys Happiness

Explanation: Some believe that financial wealth is the key to happiness. They think you'll automatically be happy once you have enough money.

Why This Myth Misleads: While money can provide comfort and security, it doesn't guarantee happiness. Happiness is more connected to relationships, purpose, and self-fulfilment than financial status. Focusing solely on money can distract from other important aspects of life.

The Truth: Money can reduce stress by covering basic needs but not ensuring emotional well-being. True happiness comes from meaningful relationships, personal growth, and a sense of purpose. Money is a tool, not the source of happiness.

Example: A millionaire who feels disconnected from family and lacks a sense of purpose may feel unfulfilled, proving that money alone doesn't create happiness.

Myth 3: Happiness Comes from Changing Everything Around You

Explanation: Many believe happiness will come if they make major changes, such as moving, switching jobs, or altering their surroundings. They think external changes will solve their inner dissatisfaction.

Why This Myth Misleads: While external changes can bring temporary relief, true happiness comes from internal peace and acceptance. Constantly seeking external solutions can prevent you from addressing the real issues within yourself. Chasing change can lead to dissatisfaction when the internal cause of unhappiness remains unresolved.

The Truth: Happiness is mainly internal, genuine and comes from within. Personal growth, self-awareness, and resilience create lasting happiness regardless of external circumstances. While external changes can help, they won't fix internal struggles.

Example: A person who constantly switches jobs in search of happiness while never addressing their lack of self-fulfilment continues to feel unsatisfied, proving that internal change is key.

Myth 4: You Must Always Be Happy

Explanation: Some believe you should strive to be happy to live a good life. This myth suggests that negative emotions have no place in a happy life.

Why This Myth Misleads: Negative emotions, like sadness or frustration, are part of the human experience. Attempting to avoid or suppress these emotions can lead to emotional exhaustion. Constantly chasing happiness can create unrealistic expectations and make every day struggles feel like failures.

The Truth: True happiness includes the ability to experience and process all positive and negative emotions. It's about balance, accepting life's challenges, and finding joy without ignoring complicated feelings. A complete emotional spectrum is key to personal growth and well-being.

Example: A person who allows themselves to feel sadness after a challenging event and later finds joy again experiences a healthier emotional balance than someone who always tries to be happy.

Myth 5: Happiness is Found in Pleasure

Explanation: Many people believe that happiness is about seeking pleasure and avoiding discomfort. They think you'll achieve happiness if you fill your life with pleasurable experiences.

Why This Myth Misleads: Pleasure is fleeting and doesn't provide long-term fulfilment. Constantly chasing pleasurable experiences can lead to emptiness and dissatisfaction when they fade. True happiness is more profound and comes from meaningful, sustained sources like relationships, purpose, and self-acceptance.

The Truth: Happiness is more than just pleasure—it's about finding joy in purpose, connection, and personal growth. Pleasure brings temporary joy, but lasting happiness comes from inner peace and living according to your values. Seeking a balance between pleasure and meaning leads to more fulfilling happiness.

Example: A person who spends all their time on short-term pleasures but feels empty afterwards learns that true happiness comes from deeper sources like family, purpose, and personal fulfilment.

Myth 6: Happiness Comes from Avoiding Conflict

Explanation: Some people think that to be happy, you need to avoid all conflicts and disagreements. They believe that conflict brings negativity and can ruin your happiness.

Why This Myth Misleads: Avoiding conflict often leads to unresolved issues and dissatisfaction. Growth, understanding, and deeper connections come from facing and resolving disputes, not avoiding them. True happiness requires healthy confrontation and problem-solving.**The Truth**: Happiness involves addressing conflicts constructively and finding resolution. Handling disagreements healthily leads to stronger relationships and personal growth. Happiness is not the absence of conflict but the ability to navigate it well.

Example: A person who avoids addressing issues with a partner may experience ongoing tension, while someone who resolves the conflict feels relief and greater happiness in the relationship.

Myth 7: Other People Have It Easier

Explanation: Many believe others have an easier path to happiness and face fewer challenges. This myth fosters a sense of comparison and unfairness.

Why This Myth Misleads: Comparing your life to others is rarely accurate, as everyone faces unseen struggles and hardships. Assuming others have it easier creates resentment and prevents you from appreciating your own journey. Happiness is personal, and each person's path is unique.

The Truth: Everyone experiences challenges, even if they aren't visible. Happiness comes from focusing on your own life and finding joy in your unique experiences rather than comparing them to others. True contentment is found when you focus on personal growth and gratitude.

Example: A person who constantly compares their life to a friend's social media posts may feel inadequate, but someone who focuses on their own achievements finds more happiness.

Myth 8: Happiness is Achieved Once and for All

Explanation: Some people believe that once you achieve happiness, it stays with you permanently. They think happiness is a final goal you reach and keep.

Why This Myth Misleads: Happiness is not a fixed state but a dynamic and fluctuating emotion. Life's ups and downs mean that happiness comes and goes, depending on circumstances. Expecting permanent happiness creates unrealistic pressure and can lead to disappointment.

The Truth: Happiness is a journey, not a destination. It's about finding joy in moments, staying resilient during difficult times, and appreciating the ebb and flow of life. True happiness is built on growth, balance, and emotional flexibility.

Example: A person who seeks happiness in achieving a big goal might feel fulfilled briefly, but happiness continues to evolve with new experiences and challenges.

Myth 9: Happiness Means No Problems

Explanation: Some believe that happiness is a life free of problems, where everything is smooth and easy. They think that happiness means never facing struggles or difficulties.

Why This Myth Misleads: Life inevitably involves challenges, and avoiding them doesn't lead to happiness. Attempting to create a problem-free life leads to frustration and avoidance. True happiness comes from resilience and the ability to navigate difficulties, not eliminate them.

The Truth: Happiness is about finding peace and joy despite life's problems, not in their absence. Overcoming challenges and building resilience are key components of lasting happiness. Growth and fulfilment often come from working through difficult situations.

Example: A person who learns to manage stress at work while maintaining a positive outlook finds more happiness than someone who avoids responsibility to prevent problems.

Myth 10: You Need a Perfect Life to Be Happy

Explanation: Some believe happiness requires a perfect life without flaws or mistakes. They think that everything must be perfect to experience true joy.

Why This Myth Misleads: Perfection is impossible to achieve, and waiting for it prevents people from enjoying the present moment. Life's imperfections and challenges are natural, and expecting everything to be perfect creates frustration and disappointment. True happiness comes from accepting and finding joy in an imperfect life.

The Truth: Happiness is about embracing life's imperfections and finding contentment in what you have. Flaws and challenges make life more meaningful, and happiness grows from appreciating your journey as it is, not waiting for perfection.

Example: A person who finds joy in their home and family, despite imperfections, feels happier than someone who is constantly dissatisfied and waits for everything to be perfect.

Myth 11: Happiness Comes from a Perfect Relationship

Explanation: Some believe that one must find and maintain a perfect relationship to be truly happy. They think happiness depends entirely on having an ideal, conflict-free partner.

Why This Myth Misleads: No relationship is perfect, and expecting perfection from a partner creates unrealistic pressures. Relationships involve growth, compromise, and challenges, all of which can strengthen bonds. Placing your happiness entirely on a relationship can led to disappointment and frustration.

The Truth: Happiness in relationships comes from mutual respect, communication, and accepting imperfections. True happiness is shared and nurtured in a relationship where both partners grow together through challenges and support. Healthy relationships are built on realistic expectations and emotional balance.

Example: A couple who accepts each other's flaws and works through disagreements finds more profound happiness than one who expects perfection and never addresses issues.

Myth 12: You Can't Be Happy Without a Partner

Explanation: Some believe that happiness is only possible if you are in a romantic relationship. They think that being single means being unfulfilled or incomplete.

Why This Myth Misleads: Happiness is an individual experience and doesn't rely on being in a relationship. While relationships can enhance happiness, they are not the sole source of it. Being content and fulfilled on your own leads to more profound happiness, whether or not you have a partner.

The Truth: True happiness comes from within and isn't dependent on your relationship status. Self-acceptance, personal growth, and a prosperous life outside relationships contribute to lasting happiness. You can find joy and fulfilment as a single person and still thrive emotionally.

Example: Someone who builds a fulfilling life through friendships, passions, and self-care feels happy and complete, even without a romantic partner.

Myth 13: Happiness Means Avoiding Negative Emotions

Explanation: Some people believe that to be happy, you must avoid feeling sadness, anger, or frustration. They think that happiness is the absence of negative emotions.

Why This Myth Misleads: Negative emotions are part of the human experience and help us grow and understand ourselves. Avoiding them can create emotional suppression, leading to more stress and dissatisfaction. Embracing negative emotions is essential for developing emotional resilience and balance.

The Truth: Happiness includes accepting and processing all emotions, not just the positive ones. Learning to deal with negative emotions healthily is a key component of overall happiness. Emotional balance, rather than avoidance, leads to more profound well-being.

Example: A person who allows themselves to feel anger or sadness when appropriate, then moves forward, experiences more balanced happiness than someone who avoids those emotions.

Myth 14: Happiness Means Constant Excitement

Explanation: Many believe that happiness comes from a life filled with excitement and adventure, always chasing new thrills. They think that without constant stimulation, life becomes dull and unhappy.

Why This Myth Misleads: Constant excitement is unsustainable and can lead to exhaustion or dissatisfaction when the thrill wears off. True happiness includes moments of peace, routine, and reflection. Chasing excitement constantly can prevent you from finding more profound, lasting joy in everyday moments.

The Truth: Happiness comes from balance, not constant high-energy excitement. It's about appreciating both the exciting moments and the calm, peaceful ones. Sustainable happiness includes finding joy in daily life, not just in big, thrilling experiences.

Example: A person who enjoys both adventurous vacations and quiet evenings at home feels more content than someone who constantly seeks out excitement and feels drained.

Myth 15: Happiness Requires Constant Optimism

Explanation: Some believe that to be truly happy, you must always maintain a positive attitude and avoid negativity. They think that negative thoughts or emotions are incompatible with happiness.

Why This Myth Misleads: Constant optimism can be unrealistic and ignores the full range of human emotions. It can also lead to emotional suppression, where people ignore real issues that need addressing. True happiness involves emotional authenticity, accepting both positive and negative emotions.

The Truth: Happiness includes allowing yourself to feel all emotions and addressing challenges honestly. Emotional balance, not forced positivity, leads to lasting happiness. Genuine happiness grows from self-compassion, resilience, and real experiences, not from constantly being optimistic.

Example: Someone who allows themselves to feel frustration during a tough day but later finds moments of joy achieves more profound happiness than someone who tries to force optimism.

Myth 16: Happiness is the Absence of Struggle

Explanation: Some believe that happiness only exists when life is easy and free of challenges. They think that struggle and happiness cannot coexist.

Why This Myth Misleads: Struggles are part of life, and avoiding them doesn't lead to happiness. Overcoming difficulties often brings more incredible achievement and fulfilment, contributing to lasting happiness. Growth and resilience come from navigating life's challenges, not avoiding them.

The Truth: Happiness is often found in overcoming struggles and growing through them. It's about developing resilience and finding joy even in difficult times. True happiness includes the ability to face challenges and emerge stronger.

Example: A person who pushes through a challenging project at work and feels a sense of pride afterwards experiences more happiness than someone who avoids the challenge.

Myth 17: Happiness Comes from External Approval

Explanation: Some believe that true happiness comes from being liked and approved of by others. They think that external validation is the key to happiness.

Why This Myth Misleads: Relying on external approval for happiness leads to insecurity and dependence on others' opinions. True happiness comes from self-acceptance and living in alignment with your values, not others' judgments. External approval is fleeting, while internal fulfilment is lasting.

The Truth: Happiness comes from within and is built on self-worth and personal values, not external validation. You create lasting emotional stability when you seek approval from yourself instead of others. True happiness grows when you live authentically without needing others' constant validation.

Example: A person who finds happiness in pursuing a career they love, despite criticism from others, feels more fulfilled than someone who constantly seeks approval from their peers.

Myth 18: Only Big Life Events Bring Happiness

Explanation: Some believe happiness comes only from major life events, such as getting married, buying a house, or achieving big goals. They think that small moments don't count toward happiness.

Why This Myth Misleads: Focusing only on big events ignores the everyday joys contributing to lasting happiness. Major events bring temporary joy but are rare, while happiness is more sustainable when you appreciate daily moments. Waiting for big events to feel happy can leave you dissatisfied in between.

The Truth: True happiness is found in appreciating the small, everyday moments as much as the big life events. Life's simple pleasures, like spending time with loved ones or enjoying a quiet afternoon, contribute to lasting happiness. Finding joy in daily life creates a more profound sense of contentment.

Example: A person who finds happiness in daily routines, like having coffee in the morning or talking with friends, feels more fulfilled than someone who only waits for significant life events to feel joy.

Myth 19: You Must Always Put Yourself First to Be Happy

Explanation: Some believe that to achieve happiness, you must prioritise your needs over others. They think that happiness requires selfishness and ignoring the needs of others.

Why This Myth Misleads: Focusing solely on yourself can lead to isolation and a lack of meaningful relationships. Happiness often comes from giving and connecting with others, not just from self-centred pursuits. Building strong connections and contributing to others' well-being often enhances personal happiness.

The Truth: Happiness grows when you balance self-care with caring for others. Meaningful relationships and acts of kindness often lead to deeper fulfilment. Putting yourself first all the time can limit your happiness while fostering connections and helping others can enrich it.

Example: A person who takes time to help a needy friend feels a sense of joy and connection, demonstrating that happiness isn't just about prioritising themselves.

Myth 20: Happiness is the Same for Everyone

Explanation: Some believe that happiness looks the same for everyone and that there's a universal formula for achieving it. They think that what makes one person happy will work for everyone.

Why This Myth Misleads: Happiness is deeply personal, and what brings joy to one person may not work for another. Everyone's path to happiness is unique and shaped by individual values, experiences, and desires. Following someone else's path to happiness can lead to frustration and dissatisfaction.

The Truth: Happiness is a personal journey, and finding what works for you is essential. True happiness comes from aligning your life with your values, passions, and goals rather than following a universal formula. It's about self-discovery and embracing what makes you happy as an individual.

Example: A person who finds joy in quiet time with a book feels fulfilled in their own way, while another person may find happiness in social gatherings, showing that happiness varies from person to person.

Myth 21: Happiness Means Escaping Reality

Explanation: Some believe that happiness comes from avoiding the pressures and responsibilities of real life. They think happiness is in escaping problems and living in a fantasy world.

Why This Myth Misleads: Escaping reality offers temporary relief and doesn't lead to lasting happiness. True happiness comes from engaging with life, facing challenges, and finding joy in the present moment. Avoiding reality can lead to deeper dissatisfaction over time.

The Truth: Happiness is rooted in embracing reality, including its imperfections and struggles. It involves finding contentment in everyday moments and building resilience to face life's challenges. Rather than avoiding it, engaging with life fully leads to deeper fulfilment.

Example: A person who finds joy in balancing their daily responsibilities with meaningful activities feels more fulfilled than someone who constantly seeks to escape through distractions like video games or TV.

4.

21 Myths about Richness

These myths primarily focused on **financial wealth**, material possessions,and misconceptions surrounding what it means to be rich. The richness myths emphasise **financial security, wealth accumulation, and lifestyle misconceptions**, not personal traits or happiness.

Myth 1: Richness is Measured by What You Own

Explanation: Some believe that the more material possessions you own—houses, cars, jewellery—the richer you are. This myth equates wealth solely with material accumulation.

Why This Myth Misleads: Owning many things doesn't necessarily make you rich; it can even cause financial strain if not managed well. True richness is about financial freedom, not just the number of possessions you have.

The Truth: Richness is measured by financial independence, security, and the ability to make choices that enhance your life. It's not about accumulating material goods but about using wealth to live meaningfully.

Example: A person with fewer material possessions but no financial debt and the freedom to travel or pursue passions feels richer than someone with lots of possessions but financial stress.

Myth 2: Richness is Only for the Lucky Few

Explanation: There's a belief that richness is only attainable by a small group of exceptionally fortunate or privileged people. This myth suggests that wealth is out of reach for most people.

Why This Myth Misleads: While certain advantages can help, many people achieve richness through determination, discipline, and financial education. Wealth-building opportunities are available to more people than this myth suggests.

The Truth: Anyone willing to learn, plan, and take action toward financial security can pursue wealth. It may require effort and strategy, but it's not reserved for a select few.

Example: A person who starts with limited resources but saves, invests, and builds wealth over time proves that richness is attainable with the right approach.

Myth 3: You Have to Inherit Wealth to Be Rich

Explanation: Some believe the only way to be truly rich is by inheriting money from wealthy parents or family. This myth limits richness to those born into wealth.

Why This Myth Misleads: Inheritance is just one pathway to financial wealth, but it's not the only one. Many people build wealth through entrepreneurship, hard work, and smart investing. Limiting richness to inheritance discourages people from pursuing wealth on their own terms.

The Truth: Richness can be created through personal effort, innovation, and disciplined financial practices. Many self-made individuals have built fortunes without inheritance, relying on creativity, persistence, and intelligent decisions.

Example: An entrepreneur who starts a small business and grows it into a profitable venture creates their own richness without relying on family wealth.

Myth 4: Richness Requires Following the Latest Financial Trends

Explanation: Some believe you must constantly chase the latest financial trends and investments to maintain or grow wealth. This myth assumes that sticking to tried-and-tested methods prevents wealth accumulation.

Why This Myth Misleads: Jumping on every new trend can lead to unnecessary risks and poor financial decisions. Consistent, long-term strategies are often more successful than chasing fads.

The Truth: Richness is often built through patience, research, and long-term investments rather than following every financial trend. Those who take a steady, well-researched approach to their finances tend to build lasting wealth.

Example: An investor who avoids trendy speculative investments and focuses on stable, diversified assets sees long-term financial growth

Myth 5: Richness Means Owning a Lot of Real Estate

Explanation: There's a common belief that wealth requires owning multiple properties and large real estate holdings. This myth equates richness with property ownership.

Why This Myth Misleads: While real estate can be a part of a wealth-building strategy, it's not the only path to richness. Many wealthy individuals diversify their investments across various asset classes and don't rely solely on property.

The Truth: Richness can be achieved through investments, including stocks, businesses, or intellectual property, not just real estate. Diversifying assets often leads to more excellent financial stability and growth.

Example: An individual who builds wealth through stocks, tech investments, and business ventures feels richer than someone who ties all their money up in property alone.

Myth 6: Richness Means Never Making Financial Sacrifices

Explanation: There's a belief that rich people never have to sacrifice anything financially—that wealth allows for constant indulgence. This myth assumes that financial choices are easy once you're wealthy.

Why This Myth Misleads: Even the wealthy need to make tough financial decisions, such as choosing between investments or managing expenses. Financial discipline is vital to maintaining wealth.

The Truth: Richness involves making calculated financial sacrifices, such as investing in long-term opportunities over short-term luxuries. Even the wealthy must prioritise and manage their financial resources.

Example: A millionaire who reinvests profits into their business instead of spending it on lavish purchases maintains long-term financial growth.

Myth 7: Richness Means You Must Have Multiple Streams of Income

Explanation: Many believe the only way to achieve true financial richness is by having multiple income streams, such as investments, businesses, and side hustles. This myth assumes that a single income source can never produce substantial wealth.

Why This Myth Misleads: While having multiple income streams can help diversify financial security, it's not the only path to richness. Many people achieve wealth through one primary source: a well-paid job, a successful business, or a high-demand skill. Quality of income, not just quantity, matters.

The Truth: Richness can come from a single, highly profitable source of income if managed well. The key is to maximise the potential of your primary income and make intelligent financial decisions, not necessarily having multiple income streams.

Example: A high-ticket coach who generates significant income from their premium coaching services builds financial richness from a single, focused business model, demonstrating that multiple income streams aren't always necessary for wealth.

Myth 8: You Can't Be Rich as an Employee

Explanation: Many believe that entrepreneurship is the only way to achieve true financial wealth and that staying an employee limits your earning potential. This myth assumes that working for someone else inherently prevents you from becoming wealthy.

Why This Myth Misleads: While entrepreneurship can lead to wealth, many employees build wealth through high-paying careers, intelligent financial management, and investing. Relying solely on entrepreneurship overlooks the potential for employees to create richness through strategic decisions.

The Truth: You can build significant wealth as an employee by negotiating for higher salaries, maximising benefits, and making wise investment decisions. Many professionals become rich by climbing the corporate ladder, leveraging stock options, or investing their income wisely.

Example: An employee who receives a high salary in a specialised field, invests their earnings in real estate or the stock market, and builds wealth over time proves that richness is not limited to entrepreneurs.

Myth 9: You Can't Be Rich if You Have Debt

Explanation: Some believe that having any form of debt prevents you from being considered rich. This myth equates debt with financial failure.

Why This Myth Misleads: Not all debt is bad—many wealthy people use leverage and smart debt (such as mortgages or business loans) to grow their wealth. Richness is about how you manage debt, not whether you have it.

The Truth: Strategic debt use can enhance wealth-building efforts, and many rich individuals carry debt as part of their financial strategies. The key is using debt responsibly to ensure it serves your long-term financial goals.

Example: An entrepreneur who takes on business loans to grow a company and generates significant returns understands that debt can contribute to richness when used wisely.

Myth 10: Richness is Only for Those Who Start Early in Life

Explanation: There's a belief that you can only become wealthy if you accumulate wealth young. This myth discourages older individuals from pursuing financial success later in life.

Why This Myth Misleads: While starting early can provide an advantage, many people build wealth later in life through careful planning, intelligent investments, and seizing new opportunities. Richness is possible at any stage of life.

The Truth: Richness can be achieved at any age through wise decisions, discipline, and consistent effort. It's never too late to start building financial security and wealth.

Example: A person who begins investing or starts a business in their 40s or 50s can still achieve significant financial richness later in life.

Myth 11: Rich People Are Always Greedy

Explanation: There's a common belief that rich people must be greedy, constantly seeking to accumulate wealth at any cost. This myth paints all wealthy people in a negative light.**Why This Myth Misleads**: Many wealthy individuals are generous and contribute significantly to society through philanthropy, mentorship, and support for causes they believe in. Associating wealth with greed creates unnecessary judgment and misunderstanding.

The Truth: Richness and generosity can coexist. Many wealthy people use their resources to make a positive impact, supporting charitable causes and helping others thrive.

Example: A business owner who donates a portion of their profits to education initiatives demonstrates that richness can be a force for good.

Myth 12: Richness is About Living Luxuriously

Explanation: Some believe wealth means living in luxury—big houses, expensive cars, designer clothes. This myth ties richness to extravagant lifestyles.

Why This Myth Misleads: An extravagant lifestyle does not guarantee richness or happiness. Focusing only on material goods can lead to financial strain and stress. Richness is about financial security and peace of mind, not just luxury.

The Truth: True richness comes from financial freedom, the ability to make choices, and the security that wealth brings, not from material excess. It's possible to be rich while living a simple, balanced life.

Example: A financially independent person who lives modestly while enjoying meaningful experiences feels richer than someone constantly chasing luxury.

Myth 13: You Can't Be Rich Working from Home

Explanation: Some believe that working from home limits one's ability to accumulate wealth, assuming one needs to be in an office or traditional business environment to achieve financial success. This myth equates remote work with lower earning potential.

Why This Myth Misleads: The rise of digital businesses, freelancing, and remote work opportunities have proven that you can build significant wealth from home. Many people, including high-ticket coaches, run highly profitable online businesses and consultancies from home.

The Truth: Richness can be achieved through remote work by leveraging digital tools, online businesses, and global opportunities. High-ticket coaches, for instance, build successful businesses offering premium coaching services to clients worldwide, all from home.

Example: An online high-ticket coach running a successful leadership coaching business, charging premium rates for one-on-one and group mentoring sessions, achieves financial richness without needing a traditional office.

Myth 14: Richness Means More Happiness

Explanation: Many people believe that once you're rich, happiness naturally follows. This myth assumes that money alone leads to emotional well-being.

Why This Myth Misleads: While wealth can provide comfort and security, it doesn't guarantee happiness. Emotional fulfilment comes from relationships, purpose, and personal growth, which money alone cannot buy.

The Truth: Richness can enhance your quality of life, but true happiness comes from meaningful connections, self-fulfilment, and inner peace. Money is just one piece of the happiness puzzle.

Example: A wealthy individual who lacks close relationships or a sense of purpose may feel unfulfilled, while someone with modest wealth but strong relationships feels truly happy.

Myth 15: Richness Guarantees Respect

Explanation: Some believe that being rich automatically earns you respect from others. This myth assumes that wealth alone commands admiration and reverence.

Why This Myth Misleads: Richness can attract attention, but respect is earned through character, actions, and how you treat others. Wealth without integrity or kindness often leads to resentment or distrust.

The Truth: True respect comes from who you are and how you contribute to the world, not just the money you have. Richness alone doesn't make people admire you—your actions and values do.

Example: A wealthy person who treats others poorly may not earn respect, while someone who uses their resources to help others gains admiration.

Myth 16: Richness Equals Power

Explanation: Some believe wealth automatically grants you influence and control over others. This myth ties wealth to dominance and authority.

Why This Myth Misleads: While wealth can provide certain advantages, true influence comes from character, relationships, and leadership. Richness doesn't automatically grant meaningful power or respect.

The Truth: Power and influence come from using your wealth to create value, build trust, and positively impact others. Richness can enhance your ability to make a difference, but respect and leadership are earned.

Example: A person who uses their wealth to empower others and support social causes gains influence through generosity and leadership, not just financial power.

Myth 17: Richness Means You Can Spend Without Limits

Explanation: Some believe that being wealthy allows you to spend as much as you want, whenever you want, without thinking about the consequences. This myth glorifies limitless spending as a sign of wealth.

Why This Myth Misleads: Even rich people must manage their finances carefully. Reckless spending can deplete wealth quickly, and financial discipline is key to maintaining richness over the long term.

The Truth: True richness is about financial control and responsibility, not just having the ability to spend. Even wealthy people must budget, invest wisely, and avoid financial pitfalls.

Example: A financially responsible individual who invests in assets instead of splurging on unnecessary luxuries maintains their richness over time.

Myth 18: Rich People Don't Have to Plan for Retirement

Explanation: There's a belief that wealthy individuals don't need to plan for retirement, assuming their current wealth will naturally sustain them. This myth suggests that financial planning for later life is unnecessary for the rich.

Why This Myth Misleads: Even rich people must plan for retirement to ensure their wealth lasts, especially considering factors like market fluctuations, lifestyle choices, and unforeseen expenses. Ignoring long-term planning can lead to financial issues later in life.

The Truth: Richness requires careful retirement planning to maintain financial stability in later years—even the wealthy need to allocate resources for retirement to secure their future and manage changing needs.

Example: A wealthy business owner who works with financial planners to ensure their well-funded retirement proves that even rich people need strategic long-term planning.

Myth 19: Rich People Have No Financial Worries

Explanation: There's a belief that once you reach a certain level of wealth, all financial worries disappear. This myth suggests that wealth automatically eliminates financial stress.

Why This Myth Misleads: Even wealthy individuals face financial concerns, such as market fluctuations, economic downturns, and managing large assets. Having money doesn't mean you're free from financial challenges.

The Truth: Rich people may still worry about maintaining their wealth, protecting their assets, or ensuring financial stability for future generations. Wealth brings different financial considerations, but not necessarily the absence of financial worries.

Example: A wealthy investor who carefully monitors market trends to protect their investments still experiences financial pressure, even with substantial wealth.

Myth 20: Rich People Are Always Satisfied with Their Wealth

Explanation: There's a belief that once someone becomes rich, they are automatically satisfied with their wealth and no longer seek more. This myth assumes that wealth always brings contentment.

Why This Myth Misleads: Many wealthy people still strive for more wealth, not necessarily out of need but out of ambition or desire for security. Richness doesn't always bring contentment, and pursuing more wealth can continue.

The Truth: Contentment is a personal mindset, not a financial state. Some wealthy people are deeply content with what they have, while others feel unsatisfied and continually chase more.

Example: A person who focuses on using wealth to create a fulfilling life experiences more contentment than someone who keeps striving for more, even after becoming wealthy.

Myth 21: Richness is About Hoarding Wealth

Explanation: Some believe that the **wealthiest** people accumulate and hold onto their wealth, never spending or sharing it. This myth glorifies the act of hoarding money.

Why This Myth Misleads: Hoarding wealth can lead to isolation, anxiety, and fear of loss. It creates a mindset of scarcity rather than abundance, preventing enjoyment of the resources you've worked hard to accumulate.

The Truth: Richness is about using wealth to enhance your life and the lives of others, not just stockpiling it. Generosity, investment, and experiences add to your richness, creating a sense of fulfilment beyond money.

Example: A person who uses their wealth to travel, donate to causes, and support their loved ones feels much more prosperous than someone who hoards money out of fear of losing it.

5.

21 Success Possibilities (SPs)

These myths primarily focused on **financial wealth**, material possessions,and misconceptions surrounding what it means to be rich. The richness myths emphasise **financial security, wealth accumulation, and lifestyle misconceptions**, not personal traits or happiness.

SP1: Passion and Success

Quadrant 1: Unpassionate and Unsuccessful

This quadrant represents those who lack both passion and success, often resulting in a lack of motivation and direction.

Example: A person working in a job they dislike without enthusiasm or effort, leading to poor performance and dissatisfaction.

Quadrant 2: Unpassionate and Successful

Here, an individual has achieved success but lacks passion, which can lead to a sense of unfulfilment.

Example: An individual who excels in their career due to technical skills but finds no joy in their work, feeling empty despite their external success.

Quadrant 3: Passionate and Unsuccessful

This quadrant is for those who are passionate but have yet to succeed. Their passion drives perseverance, but they may need more strategic direction.

Example: An artist who passionately paints struggles to sell their work due to needing more marketing knowledge or networking.

Quadrant 4: Passionate and Successful

This ideal state is where passion aligns with success, leading to fulfilment and sustained motivation.

Example: A chef who loves cooking and successfully runs a popular restaurant, combining passion with business acumen.

SP2: Motivation and Success

Quadrant 1: Lack of Motivation and Unsuccessful

This quadrant is for those who need more motivation and, as a result, do not achieve success.

Example: A student who fails to study or attend classes regularly, resulting in failing grades.

Quadrant 2: Lack of Motivation and Successful

In this quadrant, success is achieved through external pressures or routines, but the inner drive still needs to be improved.

Example: An employee who meets sales targets due to a structured work environment but feels no personal drive to excel.

Quadrant 3: Highly Motivated and Unsuccessful

Here, individuals are highly driven but unsuccessful, possibly due to poor strategy or unrealistic goals.

Example: An entrepreneur who works tirelessly on a startup but fails due to market misjudgments or lack of funding.

Quadrant 4: Highly Motivated and Successful

This is the ideal state, where high motivation, driven by internal and external factors, leads to achieving goals.

Example: A researcher passionately pursuing a cure for a disease, driven by a personal connection, and successfully making breakthroughs.

SP3: Creativity and Innovation

Quadrant 1: Lack of Creativity and Unsuccessful

This quadrant represents those who need more creativity and remain unsuccessful due to a lack of innovative thinking.

Example: A manager who strictly follows outdated processes, resulting in poor team performance and stagnation.

Quadrant 2: Lack of Creativity and Successful

In this quadrant, success is achieved through structure, discipline, or replication of proven methods rather than innovation.

Example: A franchise owner who succeeds by following a strict corporate manual without introducing any new ideas.

Quadrant 3: Highly Creative and Unsuccessful

This quadrant is for highly creative people who have yet to convert their creativity into success, possibly due to poor execution or a lack of focus.

Example: An inventor with numerous prototypes not ready for the market due to over-complicating designs without focus.

Quadrant 4: Highly Creative and Successful

This is the ideal state where creativity is effectively utilized to achieve success through innovative solutions.

Example: A tech entrepreneur who creates a successful app by blending creativity with strategic market placement.

SP4: Discipline and Consistency

Quadrant 1: Lack of Discipline and Unsuccessful

This quadrant represents those who need more discipline and consistency, leading to failure in achieving goals.

Example: A freelancer who misses deadlines due to poor time management, losing clients and income.

Quadrant 2: Lack of Discipline and Successful

This quadrant succeeds sporadically, relying on bursts of effort rather than consistent discipline.

Example: A stock trader who occasionally hits big wins but needs a structured trading strategy that can bring in consistent profits.

Quadrant 3: Highly Disciplined and Unsuccessful

This quadrant is for highly disciplined but unsuccessful people, possibly due to a rigid approach or lack of creativity.

Example: An author who writes every day without fail but needs help to get published due to not adapting to market trends.

Quadrant 4: Highly Disciplined and Successful

This is the ideal state where discipline and consistency lead to sustained success.

Example: An athlete who follows a strict training regimen and diet consistently wins competitions.

SP5: Risk-Taking and Caution

Quadrant 1: Avoids Risks and Unsuccessful

This quadrant represents those who need to be more cautious to seize opportunities, leading to missed chances for success.

Example: A business owner who refuses to invest in new technology, causing the company to fall behind its competitors.

Quadrant 2: Avoids Risks and Successful

Here, success is achieved through conservative strategies, avoiding risks that could lead to loss.

Example: An investor who only buys government bonds and accumulates wealth slowly but surely.

Quadrant 3: Takes Risks and Unsuccessful

This quadrant is for those who need more preparation or strategy to take bold risks that often lead to failure.

Example: A startup founder who invests heavily in a product without conducting market research, leading to bankruptcy.

Quadrant 4: Takes Risks and Successful

This ideal state is where calculated risks are taken wisely, leading to significant achievements.

Example: A venture capitalist who strategically invests in startups after thorough research, yielding high returns.

SP6: Work Strategies (Smart Work vs. Hard Work)

Quadrant 1: Smart Work and Unsuccessful

This quadrant represents those who employ efficient strategies but need more effort or the right circumstances to succeed.

Example: A consultant who designs effective plans but doesn't follow through with clients, resulting in minimal impact.

Quadrant 2: Smart Work and Successful

This quadrant successfully uses intelligent strategies to reach goals efficiently and effectively.

Example: A project manager who uses agile methodology to deliver projects on time and under budget.

Quadrant 3: Hard Work and Unsuccessful

Here, individuals work hard but not efficiently, which leads to burnout and minimal results.

Example: A farmer who works long hours using outdated methods and fails to maximize crop yield.

Quadrant 4: Hard Work and Successful

Despite inefficiencies, success is achieved through sheer effort and persistence.

Example: A salesperson who makes numerous cold calls daily, achieving sales through sheer volume of effort.

SP7: Perfectionism and Flexibility

Quadrant 1: Perfectionist and Unsuccessful

This quadrant represents those who strive for perfection but fail due to over-attention to detail and lack of timely execution.

Example: A designer who spends months perfecting a logo but needs to catch up on the project deadline, losing the client.

Quadrant 2: Perfectionist and Successful

Here, success is achieved through meticulous attention to detail in fields where perfection is highly valued.

Example: A surgeon known for flawless surgical procedures, earning an excellent reputation.

Quadrant 3: Flexible and Unsuccessful

This quadrant is for those who adapt frequently but need more direction or consistency, which can lead to failure to achieve goals.

Example: Entrepreneurs who constantly pivot their business model without fully committing, resulting in instability and failure.

Quadrant 4: Flexible and Successful

This is the ideal state where flexibility is used as a strength to navigate challenges and adapt to changing conditions successfully.

Example: A CEO who successfully steers the company through market downturns by quickly adapting strategies.

SP8: Emotional Intelligence (EQ) and Rational Intelligence (IQ)

Quadrant 1: Low EQ and Unsuccessful

This quadrant represents those who lack emotional intelligence, leading to poor relationships and ineffective teamwork.

Example: A manager who fails to motivate their team due to a lack of empathy and understanding.

Quadrant 2: High EQ and Unsuccessful

Here, an individual is emotionally intelligent but needs more technical skills or strategic insight to succeed.

Example: A well-liked community leader who inspires people but needs more organizational skills to execute projects effectively.

Quadrant 3: Low IQ and Successful

This quadrant is for those who succeed through emotional intelligence, leveraging strong interpersonal skills and intuition.

Example: A sales representative who builds excellent client relationships and succeeds despite having little product knowledge.

Quadrant 4: High IQ and Successful

This is the ideal state where emotional and rational intelligence combine to achieve comprehensive success.

Example: A scientist who excels in research due to high IQ and successfully manages a team due to high EQ.

SP9: Confidence and Self-Doubt

Quadrant 1: Lack of Confidence and Unsuccessful

This quadrant represents those who feel insecure and hesitant, leading to missed opportunities and underperformance.

Example: An artist who never showcases their work due to fear of criticism misses out on potential opportunities for growth and recognition.

Quadrant 2: Lack of Confidence and Successful

Here, individuals achieve success despite self-doubt, often through external validation or support.

Example: A programmer who doubts their skills but consistently delivers high-quality code, earning recognition from peers and supervisors.

Quadrant 3: High Confidence and Unsuccessful

This quadrant is for those who are overconfident but need more skills or preparation to succeed, often leading to failure.

Example: A novice trader who invests heavily without understanding the market, resulting in significant financial loss.

Quadrant 4: High Confidence and Successful

This ideal state is where confidence drives action and helps overcome challenges, leading to success.

Example: A public speaker who confidently delivers impactful speeches, gaining recognition and career advancement.

SP10: Adaptability and Stubbornness

Quadrant 1: Adaptable and Unsuccessful

This quadrant represents those who adapt frequently but need a consistent strategy, leading to unsteady progress and eventual failure.

Example: A startup founder who constantly changes their business model without allowing enough time for strategies to take hold.

Quadrant 2: Adaptable and Successful

Here, success is achieved by effectively adapting to changing environments and leveraging flexibility to overcome challenges.

Example: An educator who adjusts teaching methods to engage students better, leading to improved learning outcomes.

Quadrant 3: Stubborn and Unsuccessful

This quadrant is for those who refuse to adapt or change, resulting in stagnation and failure to capitalize on opportunities.

Example: A business owner who sticks to traditional methods despite declining sales, refusing to adopt new technology or marketing strategies.

Quadrant 4: Stubborn and Successful

This is where sticking to a proven strategy or vision leads to success through persistence and resilience.

Example: An artist who continues to produce work in their unique style despite initial rejection, eventually gaining recognition and success.

SP11: Goal Orientation (Short-Term vs. Long-Term)

Quadrant 1: Short-Term Focused and Unsuccessful

This quadrant represents those who focus on immediate gains at the expense of long-term success, often leading to burnout or quick failures.

Example: A salesperson focusing only on hitting monthly targets without building lasting client relationships experiences high turnover and inconsistency.

Quadrant 2: Short-Term Focused and Successful

Here, success is achieved through quick wins and short-term goals, but there may be a risk to sustainability and long-term growth.

Example: A trader who makes quick profits by taking advantage of market volatility but needs a long-term investment strategy.

Quadrant 3: Long-Term Focused and Unsuccessful

This quadrant is for those who prioritize long-term planning but must achieve short-term milestones, hindering overall progress.

Example: A non-profit founder with a grand vision for community impact but needs help to secure immediate funding and support.

Quadrant 4: Long-Term Focused and Successful

This is the ideal state where balancing immediate actions with long-term goals ensures sustained success and growth.

Example: A CEO who invests in employee development and innovation, resulting in steady growth and long-term company success.

SP12: Family Support and Independence

Quadrant 1: Lack of Family Support and Unsuccessful

This quadrant represents those who struggle without family support, feeling isolated and unsupported in pursuing goals.

Example: A student who cannot afford college due to a lack of financial support from family, struggling to balance work and study.

Quadrant 2: Lack of Family Support and Successful

Here, success is achieved through independence and self-reliance, finding strength in overcoming challenges.

Example: An entrepreneur who builds a business without family backing, relying on personal savings and loans to succeed.

Quadrant 3: Strong Family Support and Unsuccessful

This quadrant is for those who receive strong family support but need more personal drive or direction to translate it into success.

Example: A musician who has all the resources provided by their family but needs more dedication or skill to succeed in the industry.

Quadrant 4: Strong Family Support and Successful

This is the ideal state where strong family support is used as a foundation for achieving significant success, combining encouragement with personal effort.

Example: A student who excels academically with financial and emotional support from their family, leading to scholarships and accolades.

SP13: Connections and Networking

Quadrant 1: No Connections and Unsuccessful

This quadrant represents those needing a network and help to create opportunities or gain visibility.

Example: A freelance graphic designer with limited professional connections struggling to find clients and establish a steady stream of work.

Quadrant 2: No Connections and Successful

Here, success is achieved through personal skills, talent, or perseverance despite a lack of networking.

Example: A writer who publishes a bestseller without any industry connections, relying solely on their talent and self-promotion to reach readers.

Quadrant 3: Strong Connections and Unsuccessful

This quadrant is for those with a strong network but need to leverage it effectively, resulting in missed opportunities.

Example: An individual with many industry contacts but no meaningful collaborations or projects due to a lack of follow-through and strategic use of their network.

Quadrant 4: Strong Connections and Successful

This is the ideal state where a robust network is utilized effectively to create opportunities and achieve success.

Example: A tech entrepreneur who secures funding and partnership opportunities through a well-developed network, leveraging connections for business growth.

SP14: Physical Fitness and Energy Levels

Quadrant 1: Physically Unfit and Unsuccessful

This quadrant represents those who lack physical fitness, leading to low energy levels and poor performance.

Example: A teacher who is frequently tired and unable to engage effectively with students due to poor health habits affects their teaching quality.

Quadrant 2: Physically Unfit and Successful

Here, individuals achieve success despite physical challenges, often relying on mental resilience or external support.

Example: A writer who produces excellent work despite chronic health issues, using inner strength and mental focus to overcome physical limitations.

Quadrant 3: Physically Fit and Unsuccessful

This quadrant is for those physically fit but lacking the focus or strategy needed to succeed.

Example: An athlete in top physical shape fails to perform better due to poor mental preparation or lack of strategic planning.

Quadrant 4: Physically Fit and Successful

This ideal state is where physical fitness is leveraged to maintain high energy levels, focus, and performance, leading to success.

Example: A corporate executive who maintains a rigorous fitness routine, which enhances their productivity and leadership capabilities.

SP15: Financial Stability and Stress

Quadrant 1: Financially Unstable and Unsuccessful

This quadrant represents those who lack financial stability, leading to high stress and an inability to focus on long-term goals.

Example: A recent graduate with significant student debt, struggling to find a job and manage their finances, unable to plan for the future.

Quadrant 2: Financially Unstable and Successful

Here, success is achieved despite financial instability, often through creativity or risk-taking.

Example: A startup founder who operates on a tight budget but manages to grow the business through innovative solutions and sheer determination.

Quadrant 3: Financially Stable and Unsuccessful

This quadrant is for those with financial stability who need more drive or strategy to succeed.

Example: A trust fund beneficiary who is financially secure but fails to pursue meaningful personal or professional goals, leading to a lack of fulfilment.

Quadrant 4: Financially Stable and Successful

This is the ideal state where financial stability supports strategic risk-taking and long-term planning, leading to success.

Example: An investor who uses their financial cushion to take calculated risks, resulting in high returns and growth.

SP16: Access to Resources and Resourcefulness

Quadrant 1: Lack of Resources and Unsuccessful

This quadrant represents those who lack resources and struggle to find ways to compensate, leading to stagnation.

Example: A small business owner needs help to secure funding or resources, resulting in limited growth and eventual closure.

Quadrant 2: Lack of Resources and Successful

Here, success is achieved through creativity and resourcefulness, finding ways to make do with what is available.

Example: A filmmaker creating a successful indie movie on a shoestring budget using innovative techniques and crowd-sourced talent.

Quadrant 3: Abundant Resources and Unsuccessful

This quadrant is for those with access to ample resources. Still, they fail to use them effectively, resulting in missed opportunities.

Example: A tech company with significant funding but no clear product strategy, leading to wasted resources and market failure.

Quadrant 4: Abundant Resources and Successful

This is the ideal state where available resources are used effectively to maximize opportunities and achieve success.

Example: A non-profit organization with solid donor support that uses its funds strategically to make a significant impact and achieve its mission.

SP17: Cultural Expectations and Personal Values

Quadrant 1: Conform to Cultural Expectations and Unsuccessful

This quadrant represents those who follow cultural norms but fail to succeed personally or professionally.

Example: A corporate employee who strictly adheres to company culture but needs more creativity, resulting in limited career progression and personal fulfilment.

Quadrant 2: Conform to Cultural Expectations and Successful

Here, success is achieved by aligning actions with cultural expectations and societal norms.

Example: A lawyer who follows the traditional career path and excels within the firm, gaining promotions and recognition by adhering to established norms.

Quadrant 3: Defy Cultural Expectations and Unsuccessful

This quadrant is for those who challenge norms but struggle to gain acceptance or succeed.

Example: An artist who rejects conventional art forms and faces constant criticism, struggling to gain a following and recognition in the art world.

Quadrant 4: Defy Cultural Expectations and Successful

This is the ideal state where success is achieved by staying true to personal values and challenging societal norms.

Example: A social entrepreneur who builds a successful enterprise by prioritizing social impact over profit, gaining widespread acclaim for their innovative approach.

SP18: Workplace Environment (Toxic vs. Supportive)

Quadrant 1: Toxic Environment and Unsuccessful

This quadrant represents those who work in a hostile environment, leading to stress, burnout, and failure to achieve goals.

Example: A software developer who leaves a toxic workplace where innovation is stifled and management is unsupportive, resulting in career setbacks.

Quadrant 2: Toxic Environment and Successful

Here, success is achieved despite a toxic environment through resilience and personal drive.

Example: A journalist who wins awards despite working in a newsroom filled with tension and competition, demonstrating strength and perseverance.

Quadrant 3: Supportive Environment and Unsuccessful

This quadrant is for those who work in a positive environment but fail to leverage the support to succeed.

Example: A marketing executive in a nurturing company culture who needs more initiative, leading to career stagnation despite the supportive environment.

Quadrant 4: Supportive Environment and Successful

This is the ideal state where a positive work environment is leveraged to foster collaboration and achieve success.

Example: A researcher who makes groundbreaking discoveries thanks to a collaborative, supportive lab environment that encourages innovation.

SP19: Mentorship and Guidance

Quadrant 1: No Mentorship and Unsuccessful

This quadrant represents those who need more mentorship and guidance, leading to a lack of direction and underachievement.

Example: A young professional who needs a mentor to navigate career growth, making numerous mistakes and missing opportunities.

Quadrant 2: No Mentorship and Successful

Success is achieved through self-teaching, personal experiences, and trial and error.

Example: A self-taught coder who builds a successful app and gains recognition without formal mentorship, relying on personal initiative and learning.

Quadrant 3: Strong Mentorship and Unsuccessful

This quadrant is for those with access to mentors who need help applying advice or effectively leveraging guidance.

Example: A graduate student who receives valuable advice from a mentor but doesn't implement the feedback, leading to poor research outcomes.

Quadrant 4: Strong Mentorship and Successful

This is the ideal state where mentorship is utilized effectively to learn, grow, and achieve career or personal success.

Example: A junior architect who thrives under the guidance of a senior mentor, leading to rapid career advancement and professional recognition.

SP20: Market Conditions and Timing

Quadrant 1: Poor Market Conditions and Unsuccessful

This quadrant represents those who operate in a challenging market environment, leading to failure despite efforts.

Example: A retail store owner who opens a business during an economic recession faces low sales and high debts and struggles to sustain the business.

Quadrant 2: Poor Market Conditions and Successful

Here, success is achieved despite unfavourable market conditions through innovation or niche focus.

Example: A home-based crafts business that thrives during an economic downturn by selling unique, affordable products online, capitalizing on niche demand.

Quadrant 3: Favorable Market Conditions and Unsuccessful

This quadrant is for those who fail to capitalize on a booming market, resulting in missed opportunities.

Example: A tech startup that doesn't innovate or adapt despite a growing demand for its product type, leading to stagnation and lost potential.

Quadrant 4: Favorable Market Conditions and Successful

This is the ideal state where a favourable market environment is fully leveraged to achieve significant success.

Example: A solar energy company that rapidly expands during a surge in demand for renewable energy solutions, taking full advantage of the market conditions.

SP21: Technology Utilization and Digital Savviness

Quadrant 1: Low-Tech Utilization and Unsuccessful

This quadrant represents those who need more digital skills or fail to adopt technology, leading to inefficiency and an inability to compete.

Example: A traditional bookstore that needs to develop an online presence, losing business to e-commerce giants that dominate the market.

Quadrant 2: Low-Tech Utilization and Successful

Here, success is achieved despite minimal technology use, often through high-quality, personalised service or a niche focus.

Example: A bespoke tailor who builds a strong clientele through word-of-mouth and personalised service, succeeding with a minimal digital presence.

Quadrant 3: High-Tech Utilization and Unsuccessful

This quadrant is for those who embrace technology but need help to use it strategically, resulting in inefficiency and failure.

Example: A new restaurant that invests heavily in digital marketing without a clear target audience, resulting in low customer turnout and wasted resources.

Quadrant 4: High-Tech Utilization and Successful

This is the ideal state where technology and digital tools are used effectively to enhance operations, marketing, and customer engagement.

Example: An online fitness coach who leverages social media and virtual training platforms to build a global client base, effectively reaching a broad audience.

6.

6 Additional Success Possibilities

SP22: Resilience and Vulnerability

Quadrant 1: Low Resilience and Unsuccessful

This quadrant represents those who struggle to bounce back from setbacks, leading to prolonged failure or quitting.

Example: A musician who gives up after receiving negative feedback, never attempting to perform again due to a lack of resilience.

Quadrant 2: High Resilience and Unsuccessful

Here, individuals show resilience but need more strategy or resources to succeed despite their persistent efforts.

Example: An activist who continues campaigning for a cause despite ongoing setbacks and little progress, demonstrating resilience without strategic impact.

Quadrant 3: Low Resilience and Successful

This quadrant is for those who achieve success but may lack the emotional strength to handle failure or setbacks gracefully.

Example: A young athlete who wins easily but quits the sport after losing their first major competition, unable to cope with the disappointment.

Quadrant 4: High Resilience and Successful

This is the ideal state where resilience is combined with strategy and adaptability to achieve and sustain success.

Example: A business leader who turns a company around after multiple crises, demonstrating resilience and strategic insight.

SP23: Stress Management and Well-being

Quadrant 1: Poor Stress Management and Unsuccessful

This quadrant represents those who poorly manage stress, leading to burnout and failure to achieve goals.

Example: A journalist who misses deadlines due to stress-induced health issues ultimately loses their job because of poor stress management.

Quadrant 2: Poor Stress Management and Successful

Here, success is achieved at the cost of personal well-being and long-term health.

Example: A high-powered lawyer who wins many cases but suffers from chronic stress and health problems pays a high personal price for their success.

Quadrant 3: Excellent Stress Management and Unsuccessful

This quadrant is for those who manage stress well but lack the drive or strategy to succeed.

Example: A mid-level employee who enjoys a good work-life balance but remains stagnant in their career due to a lack of ambition or goals.

Quadrant 4: Excellent Stress Management and Successful

This is the ideal state where success is achieved while maintaining well-being and balance, effectively managing stress.

Example: A company executive who practices mindfulness and delegation to maintain productivity and personal health, achieving a balanced and successful career.

SP24: Decision-Making Styles (Analytical vs. Intuitive)

Quadrant 1: Analytical Decision-Maker and Unsuccessful

This quadrant represents those who rely heavily on data and analysis but are paralyzed by overthinking and missing opportunities.

Example: An investor who constantly analyses market data but never makes a timely decision, resulting in missed profitable trades.

Quadrant 2: Analytical Decision-Maker and Successful

Here, success is achieved by effectively using data and analysis to make informed decisions.

Example: A supply chain manager who uses data analytics to optimize logistics, reduce costs, and increase efficiency, demonstrating the power of analytical thinking.

Quadrant 3: Intuitive Decision-Maker and Unsuccessful

This quadrant is for those who make decisions based on gut feelings, sometimes leading to misjudgement and failure.

Example: A fashion retailer who stocks based on personal taste rather than customer demand, resulting in unsold inventory and financial losses.

Quadrant 4: Intuitive Decision-Maker and Successful

This is the ideal state where intuition and quick thinking are successfully relied upon to make impactful decisions.

Example: A serial entrepreneur who trusts their instincts to make bold, innovative moves, leading to multiple business successes.

SP25: Work-Life Integration and Personal Fulfilment

Quadrant 1: Poor Integration and Unsuccessful

This quadrant represents those who fail to balance personal and professional life, resulting in burnout and dissatisfaction.

Example: A doctor who works long hours, neglecting family and personal health, leading to professional mistakes and personal regrets.

Quadrant 2: Poor Integration and Successful

Here, individuals achieve career success at the cost of personal relationships and well-being.

Example: A CEO who builds a successful company but has no time for family or personal life, leading to loneliness and isolation.

Quadrant 3: Good Integration and Unsuccessful

This quadrant is for those who maintain an excellent personal-professional balance but fail to succeed professionally.

Example: A graphic designer who enjoys a balanced life but struggles to find high-paying clients or meaningful projects, limiting their career growth.

Quadrant 4: Good Integration and Successful

Work and personal life are balanced effectively in this ideal state, leading to personal fulfilment and professional success.

Example: A consultant who schedules time for family and hobbies while maintaining a thriving client base and business growth, achieving harmony in life.

SP26: Purpose and Meaning

Quadrant 1: Lack of Purpose and Unsuccessful

This quadrant represents those who need a clear purpose, resulting in aimlessness and failure to achieve meaningful success.

Example: A college graduate who takes various jobs without clear career goals, feeling unfulfilled and underachieving in their professional life.

Quadrant 2: Lack of Purpose and Successful

Here, success is achieved regarding status or wealth but feels unfulfilling due to a lack of deeper meaning.

Example: A corporate lawyer who makes a high salary but feels disconnected from their work and its impact, struggling with a sense of emptiness.

Quadrant 3: Clear Purpose and Unsuccessful

This quadrant is for those with a strong sense of purpose. Still, they need help translating it into concrete success due to various obstacles.

Example: A social worker who is deeply committed to helping people experiencing homelessness faces systemic barriers and limited resources, making progress difficult.

Quadrant 4: Clear Purpose and Successful

This ideal state is where a strong sense of purpose is aligned with actions, leading to personal fulfilment and professional success.

Example: A non-profit founder who successfully drives change in their community, feeling deeply connected to their mission and accomplishments.

SP27: Introversion vs. Extroversion in Success

Quadrant 1: Introvert and Unsuccessful

This quadrant represents those who prefer solitude and struggle with networking or self-promotion, hindering their success.

Example: An IT specialist who excels technically but fails to get promotions due to a lack of visibility and networking within the company.

Quadrant 2: Introvert and Successful

Here, success is achieved by leveraging strengths like deep focus, listening, and thoughtful decision-making.

Example: A novelist who writes best-selling books by working in quiet solitude, excelling without needing constant social interaction.

Quadrant 3: Extrovert and Unsuccessful

This quadrant is for those who engage socially but need more focus or depth, which is required for sustained success.

Example: A salesperson who networks extensively but fails to close deals due to a lack of detailed product knowledge and follow-through.

Quadrant 4: Extrovert and Successful

This ideal state is where social skills, charisma, and networking are used to build strong relationships and achieve goals.

Example: A politician who wins elections through strong public speaking skills, networking, and the ability to engage voters effectively, achieving success in their field.

7.

21 Success Evaluation Questions (SEQs)

Success isn't a destination—it's a journey filled with continuous learning, reflection, and growth. In this journey, it's crucial to regularly assess where you stand and what changes might be needed to keep moving forward effectively. This is where **Success Evaluation Questions (SEQs)** come into play.

What are SEQs?

Success Evaluation Questions, or SEQs, are thoughtfully designed prompts encouraging introspection and self-assessment. These questions act as mirrors, reflecting your strengths and areas for improvement. Regularly engaging with SEQs can provide deeper insights into your habits, beliefs, and behaviours that either propel you toward your goals or hold you back.

Why SEQs Matter:

1. **Self-Reflection:** SEQs allow you to pause and reflect on your actions, decisions, and mindset. They encourage you to look inward, fostering a deeper understanding of your personal and professional journey.
2. **Identify Growth Opportunities:** These questions help pinpoint areas where you may need to shift your focus, improve your skills, or change your approach. They highlight the gaps between where you are and where you want to be.
3. **Cultivate Self-Awareness:** By regularly considering SEQs, you cultivate self-awareness—a crucial component of emotional intelligence. Understanding your motivations, strengths, and weaknesses enables you to navigate challenges more effectively.
4. **Encourage Action:** SEQs are not just about reflection; they are also about action. They push you to think about what you can do differently, what steps you need to take, and how you can better align your actions with your goals and values.
5. **Promote Accountability:** Engaging with SEQs fosters a sense of personal accountability. Regularly evaluating your progress and

decisions makes you responsible for your growth and achievements.

How to Use SEQs:

- **Daily or Weekly Reflection:** Set aside time each day or week to review a few SEQs. Reflect on your answers honestly and without judgment. This practice will help you align with your goals and make necessary adjustments.
- **Journaling:** Write down your responses to each SEQ in a journal. Over time, this will create a valuable record of your growth and transformation, offering insights into how far you've come and what still needs attention.
- **Goal Setting and Review:** Incorporate SEQs into your goal-setting process. Use them to clarify your objectives and evaluate your progress. Regularly review your answers to see if you're moving in the right direction.
- **Group Discussions or Mentoring:** SEQs can also be used in group settings or mentoring relationships. Discussing these questions with peers or mentors can provide diverse perspectives and deepen your understanding.

Integrating SEQs into your routine is a powerful tool for continuous improvement and success. Remember, the path to success is not about perfection but about progress. Use these questions to stay curious, committed, and on course.

SEQ 1: You set goals that match your passion.

Why It Matters:

Setting clear, achievable goals forms the foundation of success. Goals provide direction, motivation, and a sense of purpose. When these goals align with your passion, they become even more powerful, driving you to achieve things that genuinely matter to you. Passion fuels your persistence, and clear goals offer the roadmap.

What to Reflect On:

- Do you take the time to define your goals clearly?
- Are your goals specific, measurable, and time-bound?
- Do your goals reflect your passion, or do external pressures influence them?
- How often do you revisit and adjust your goals to align with your evolving passions?

Answering YES Indicates that you proactively shape your path to success and are likely on a fulfilling journey.

Answering NO suggests a need for investing more time in goal setting and ensuring that those goals align with what you truly care about.

SEQ 2: You make your luck by acting every day.

Why It Matters:

Luck often results from consistent action and preparation rather than something random. By taking consistent, focused action, you position yourself where opportunities can arise. The more proactive you are, the "luckier" you seem to get.

What to Reflect On:

- Are you consistently taking steps toward your goals, even when progress seems slow?
- Do you seize opportunities when they arise or let them pass by?
- How do you prepare yourself for potential opportunities—through learning, networking, or adaptability?
- Do you believe your actions significantly impact the outcomes you experience?

Answering YES: Indicates that you actively participate in your success, understanding that luck often comes to those who prepare.

Answering NO suggests that you might be waiting for success to come to you rather than actively creating it through your actions.

SEQ 3: You focus on tasks that make a big impact.

Why It Matters:

Focusing on high-impact tasks is a hallmark of effective leadership. When you concentrate on the actions that matter most, you maximize your influence and ensure progress towards your significant goals. These tasks often yield more excellent results, increase your productivity, and allow you to make meaningful contributions in your field. Success is not about doing everything but the right things that push the needle forward.

What to Reflect On:

- Do you prioritize tasks that will make the most significant difference in achieving your goals?
- Are you clear which activities offer the highest return on your time and effort?
- Do you delegate low-impact tasks to create more room for impactful actions?
- How do you stay focused on what matters most, avoiding distractions?

Answering YES: Indicates that you understand the value of focusing on impactful activities and are likely to see faster progress and more excellent results in your endeavours.

Answering NO suggests a need for refining your focus, delegating less critical tasks, and concentrating on what drives real results.

SEQ 4: You lead with vision, steering your way to success.

Why It Matters:

Leadership without vision is like sailing without a compass. A clear vision provides direction, purpose, and long-term goals, guiding you and your team towards success. Visionary leadership inspires others to join you, creating alignment and motivation. When you lead with vision, you become proactive, steering your efforts towards a future you consciously shape rather than reacting to circumstances.

What to Reflect On:

- Do you envision where you want to go, personally and professionally?
- Are your daily actions aligned with this vision, moving you closer to your long-term goals?
- How effectively do you communicate your vision to others, inspiring and guiding them toward shared objectives?
- Do you regularly reassess your vision to ensure it remains relevant and achievable?

Answering YES: Indicates that you are a forward-thinking leader, consistently steering yourself and others toward meaningful success.

Answering NO suggests you must invest time crafting a clear vision and aligning your actions with your desired future.

SEQ 5: You embrace risk, knowing it leads to success.

Why It Matters:

Success often requires stepping outside of your comfort zone and taking calculated risks. Embracing risk is about recognizing that opportunities usually come with uncertainty, and avoiding risk can mean missing out on growth and success. Leaders who understand this see risk not as a threat but as a necessary component of innovation and achievement. By embracing risk, you open yourself to new possibilities and breakthroughs that can lead to extraordinary results.

What to Reflect On:

- Do you take calculated risks that align with your goals or play them safe?
- How do you assess risks and prepare for potential challenges?
- Are you comfortable with uncertainty, knowing it often leads to growth and success?
- How do you manage your fear of failure while taking risks that could bring big rewards?

Answering YES indicates that you understand the role of risk in achieving success and are willing to take a chance on uncertainty for greater rewards.

Answering NO suggests you may be holding back from potential opportunities and could benefit from evaluating how strategic risk-taking can accelerate your success.

SEQ 6: You keep learning.

Why It Matters:

Continuous learning is the foundation of long-term success. Adapting, growing, and evolving through learning is crucial in a rapidly changing world. Leaders who commit to lifelong learning stay ahead of the curve, discovering new strategies, skills, and perspectives that keep them relevant and effective. Learning fuels innovation, keeps you adaptable, and ensures you're constantly improving personally and professionally.

What to Reflect On:

- Do you actively seek new knowledge and skills to stay ahead in your field?
- Are you open to learning from failures, challenges, and even from others around you?
- How do you integrate learning into your daily routine, ensuring continuous growth?
- Do you prioritize learning as a critical part of your personal and professional development?

Answering YES: Indicates that you value growth and view learning as essential for ongoing success.

Answering NO suggests you might be limiting your potential and could benefit from prioritizing continuous learning to unlock more outstanding achievements.

SEQ 7: You align your values with your actions.

Why It Matters:

When your actions reflect your core values, you create a sense of integrity and purpose that drives lasting success. Alignment between values and actions builds trust, fosters confidence, and creates a sense of fulfilment in both personal and professional life. Leaders who operate from a place of authenticity inspire others and maintain a strong sense of direction, ensuring their success is measurable and meaningful.

What to Reflect On:

- Do your daily actions reflect the values you hold dear?
- How do you ensure your decisions align with personal and professional principles?
- Are you willing to stand by your values, even when it's challenging or inconvenient?
- How does living in alignment with your values enhance your overall sense of success and satisfaction?

Answering YES indicates that you lead with integrity and purpose and will likely experience success and fulfilment.

Answering NO suggests that you must evaluate how your actions align with your core values, ensuring that you lead from a place of authenticity and purpose.

SEQ 8: You frequently overlook self-awareness.

Why It Matters:

Self-awareness is a cornerstone of effective leadership and personal growth. Without it, you may fail to recognize your strengths and weaknesses and how your behaviour impacts others. Highly self-aware leaders make better decisions, build stronger relationships, and continuously improve. Overlooking self-awareness can lead to missed opportunities for growth and misaligned actions.

What to Reflect On:

- Do you take time to reflect on your actions and their effects on others?
- How often do you assess your strengths and areas for improvement?
- Are you open to feedback, and do you use it to become more self-aware?
- How could increasing self-awareness enhance your leadership and personal success?

Answering YES Indicates that you may neglect self-awareness, limiting your ability to grow and lead effectively.

Answering NO: Suggest prioritising self-awareness and positioning yourself for continuous growth and success.

SEQ 9: You prioritize achievement over personal development.

Why It Matters:

Focusing solely on achievement can lead to burnout and a lack of fulfilment. Personal development, on the other hand, provides the foundation for sustainable success. Leaders who invest in personal growth build resilience, creativity, and adaptability, fueling long-term achievement. When you prioritize personal development, you grow as a person and a leader, ultimately driving better results.

What to Reflect On:

- Do you focus more on achieving external goals than on your personal growth?
- How often do you invest in learning new skills, improving your mindset, or developing your character?
- Are you balancing your ambition with efforts to become a better version of yourself?
- How could shifting focus toward personal development help you achieve lasting success?

Answering YES indicates that you may be sacrificing personal development for short-term achievement, which could limit your long-term growth.

Answering NO suggests that you're actively balancing achievement with personal growth, ensuring sustained success and fulfilment.

SEQ 10: You tend to dismiss unfamiliar ideas.

Why It Matters:

Dismissing unfamiliar ideas can limit your potential for innovation, growth, and success. New ideas often lead to breakthroughs, offering fresh perspectives and solutions you might not have considered. Leaders who are open to unfamiliar concepts are more adaptable, creative, and effective in solving problems. By embracing new ideas, even when they challenge your existing beliefs, you open yourself to greater possibilities and progress.

What to Reflect On:

- Do you resist ideas that feel unfamiliar or outside your comfort zone?
- How often do you actively explore new perspectives or concepts that challenge your thinking?
- Are you open to learning from others who think differently, even when their ideas are unconventional?
- How could being more receptive to unfamiliar ideas spark innovation and accelerate your success?

Answering YES indicates that you may be limiting your opportunities for growth by dismissing unfamiliar ideas and could benefit from embracing a more open mindset.

Answering NO suggests that you are open to exploring new ideas and perspectives, positioning yourself for greater creativity and success in your endeavours.

SEQ 11: You frequently need more consistent practice.

Why It Matters:

Consistent practice is the key to mastery and long-term success. Without regular effort, skills stagnate, and progress slows. Whether honing a skill, building a habit, or achieving a goal, consistency transforms potential into results. Leaders who commit to steady, intentional practice are likelier to achieve excellence and set a strong example for others.

What to Reflect On:

- Do you practice your skills or work toward your goals regularly, or is it sporadic?
- How often do you dedicate time to deliberate practice, focusing on areas that need improvement?
- Are you committed to consistency, even when progress seems slow or challenging?
- How could a more consistent practice routine accelerate your growth and bring you closer to success?

Answering YES: You may need to establish consistency in your practice to ensure steady improvement and progress.

Answering NO suggests you are likely committed to consistent practice, setting yourself up for mastery and success.

SEQ 12: You lack hope in being resilient in adversity.

Why It Matters:

Resilience is the ability to bounce back from challenges, a crucial trait for long-term success. Without hope in your ability to be resilient, setbacks can feel overwhelming, and you may struggle to overcome adversity. Hope fuels resilience, giving you the strength to persevere even in tough times. Leaders who believe in their capacity to navigate difficulties inspire others and are more likely to turn challenges into opportunities for growth.

What to Reflect On:

- Do you believe in overcoming obstacles or feel defeated by challenges?
- How do you typically respond to setbacks—do you see them as temporary or insurmountable?
- Are you actively building habits and mental strength to increase your resilience?
- How could developing hope in your resilience change how you face adversity and help you succeed?

Answering YES indicates that you may struggle to be confident in your resilience and could benefit from cultivating hope and strategies for overcoming adversity.

Answering NO suggests that you possess strong resilience, enabling you to confidently navigate challenges and emerge stronger on the other side.

SEQ 13: You keep fearing the unknown.

Why It Matters:

Fear of the unknown can hold you back from seizing new opportunities, taking calculated risks, and embracing change. Leaders who face uncertainty with courage and curiosity often unlock new pathways to success. While the unknown can feel intimidating, it's also where growth and innovation thrive. By overcoming this fear, you empower yourself to explore new possibilities, adapt to change, and achieve greater accomplishments.

What to Reflect On:

- Do you let fear of the unknown prevent you from taking risks or exploring new things?
- How often do you step out of your comfort zone to embrace change and uncertainty?
- Are you willing to face challenges without knowing the exact outcome, trusting your ability to adapt?
- How could overcoming your fear of the unknown open more growth and success opportunities?

Answering YES indicates that your fear of uncertainty may be limiting your potential. Facing the unknown with confidence could lead to personal and professional breakthroughs.

Answering NO suggests that you are willing to embrace the unknown, positioning yourself for growth, adaptability, and future success.

SEQ 14: You avoid conflict resolution.

Why It Matters:

Avoiding conflict resolution can lead to unresolved issues, strained relationships, and missed opportunities for growth. Conflict can strengthen teams, improve communication, and lead to creative solutions when handled effectively. Leaders who confront conflicts head-on build trust, create more open environments, and foster stronger relationships. Avoiding conflict only allows problems to fester, making success more challenging in the long run.

What to Reflect On:

- Do you actively address conflicts when they arise, or do you tend to avoid them?
- How often do you seek constructive solutions when disagreements occur instead of letting tension build?
- Are you comfortable with difficult conversations that can lead to better outcomes?
- How could improving your conflict resolution skills enhance your relationships and leadership effectiveness?

Answering YES: Indicates that you may be missing growth opportunities and relationship-building by avoiding conflict resolution.

Answering NO suggests that you are proactive in resolving conflicts, which can lead to stronger connections and a healthier, more successful environment.

SEQ 15: You need more preparation.

Why It Matters:

Preparation is the foundation of success. Even the most talented individuals can fall short of their potential without proper preparation. Being well-prepared allows you to anticipate challenges, seize opportunities, and confidently navigate uncertainty. Leaders who prioritize preparation set themselves and their teams up for success by ensuring they have the knowledge, skills, and resources necessary to achieve their goals.

What to Reflect On:

- Do you regularly prepare thoroughly before taking on new challenges or projects?
- How often do you invest time in research, planning, and practice to ensure success?
- Are you proactive in identifying potential obstacles and creating strategies to overcome them?
- How could better preparation improve your performance and outcomes in both personal and professional settings?

Answering YES Indicates that you may need to invest more time and effort into preparation to ensure that you're ready to tackle challenges effectively.

Answering NO suggests that you already prioritise preparation, setting yourself up for success and minimizing surprises.

SEQ 16: You avoid building meaningful connections.

Why It Matters:

Meaningful connections are essential for personal and professional success. Leaders who foster strong relationships have access to support, collaboration, and new perspectives. Avoiding the effort to build these connections can leave you isolated and limit your ability to grow and succeed. Building relationships strengthens your leadership, opens opportunities, and creates a network that provides guidance, feedback, and encouragement.

What to Reflect On:

- Do you invest time and energy in building meaningful connections with others?
- How often do you engage with people on a deeper level rather than just surface interactions?
- Are you willing to reach out and nurture relationships, even when it's not easy?
- How could focusing on building connections expand your opportunities for personal and professional growth?

Answering YES indicates that you may neglect the importance of meaningful connections, which could hinder your success.

Answering NO suggests that you actively build and nurture relationships, positioning yourself for greater success and collaboration.

SEQ 17: You frequently blame external factors.

Why It Matters:

Blaming external factors shifts responsibility away from you, limiting your control over your success. When you focus on external circumstances rather than what you can change, you give away your power to influence outcomes. Leaders who take ownership of their actions and decisions understand that while external factors may play a role, personal responsibility is key to growth and success. Shifting your mindset from blame to ownership allows you to take control and create the results you desire.

What to Reflect On:

- Do you frequently blame circumstances, people, or situations for setbacks?
- How often do you take responsibility for your role in the outcomes you experience?
- Are you willing to focus on what you can control rather than what is beyond your control?
- How could taking more ownership of your actions and decisions accelerate your growth and success?

Answering YES Indicates that blaming external factors may be holding you back, and shifting to a mindset of ownership could empower you to make meaningful progress.

Answering NO suggests that you are already taking responsibility for your actions and outcomes and positioning yourself for growth and success.

SEQ 18: You often compare yourself with others.

Why It Matters:

Constantly comparing yourself to others can diminish your confidence, increase stress, and distract you from your unique path to success. Everyone's journey is different, and focusing on others can prevent you from recognizing your progress and strengths. Leaders who concentrate on personal growth rather than comparisons achieve greater satisfaction and maintain a clearer sense of purpose. Success comes from improving yourself, not measuring yourself against others.

What to Reflect On:

- Do you frequently measure your success based on how others are performing?
- How often do comparisons make you feel less accomplished or confident?
- Are you focusing on your personal growth and unique journey instead of worrying about what others are doing?
- How could letting go of comparisons help you focus on your strengths and accelerate your success?

Answering YES indicates that comparing yourself to others may be holding you back, and shifting your focus to personal growth could lead to greater fulfilment and success.

Answering NO suggests that you prioritise your journey, which positions you for sustained growth and achievement without the distraction of external comparisons.

SEQ 19: You tend to avoid discomfort.

Why It Matters:

Avoiding discomfort limits your growth and prevents you from reaching your full potential. Discomfort often accompanies the process of learning, adapting, and improving. Leaders who embrace discomfort understand that it's a necessary part of progress and success. By stepping outside your comfort zone, you unlock new opportunities, build resilience, and strengthen your ability to handle challenges effectively.

What to Reflect On:

- Do you shy away from situations that make you uncomfortable, even if they lead to growth?
- How often do you challenge yourself to step outside your comfort zone and face new experiences?
- Are you willing to embrace discomfort as part of your personal and professional development?
- How could pushing past discomfort help you achieve tremendous success and build confidence?

Answering YES indicates that avoiding discomfort may hinder your growth, but embracing it could unlock new opportunities and lead to greater success.

Answering NO suggests that you understand the value of discomfort in personal and professional growth, positioning yourself for continuous improvement and achievement.

SEQ 20: You often need more communication.

Why It Matters:

Effective communication is the cornerstone of successful leadership and collaboration. When communication is lacking, misunderstandings arise, relationships suffer, and goals may be missed. Leaders who communicate clearly and frequently build stronger teams, foster trust, and ensure alignment toward shared objectives. By improving communication, you create an open environment where ideas flow freely and everyone is on the same page, paving the way for tremendous success.

What to Reflect On:

- Do you often find that your thoughts or ideas are not communicated to others?
- How frequently do you communicate openly and transparently with those around you?
- Are you actively seeking feedback and ensuring that your messages are understood?
- How could improving your communication skills strengthen your leadership and help you achieve more effective results?

Answering YES, you may need to invest more in communication to ensure clarity, collaboration, and alignment.

Answering NO suggests that you prioritise communication, enabling you to build strong relationships and achieve better outcomes through clear and compelling interactions.

SEQ 21: You regularly cling to your comfort zones.

Why It Matters:

Clinging to your comfort zone restricts your growth and limits your potential for success. While staying in familiar surroundings may feel safe, progress happens when you push yourself beyond what is comfortable. Leaders who embrace new challenges and step outside their comfort zones are more adaptable, innovative, and resilient. Letting go of your comfort zone creates opportunities for personal development and long-term success.

What to Reflect On:

- Do you avoid taking risks or exploring new things because they take you out of your comfort zone?
- How often do you challenge yourself with tasks or experiences that stretch your abilities?
- Are you willing to embrace uncertainty and discomfort to grow?
- How could breaking free from your comfort zone lead to new opportunities and accelerate your success?

Answering YES Indicates that clinging to your comfort zone may be holding you back, and stepping out could unlock new possibilities and personal growth.

Answering NO suggests that you are already up for regularly challenging yourself and positioning yourself for continuous learning and more remarkable achievements.

8.

6 Additional Success Evaluation Questions

SEQ 22: You hesitate to act when uncertain.

Why It Matters:

Uncertainty is a constant in leadership and life. Waiting for complete certainty can lead to missed opportunities, while decisive action in the face of uncertainty drives progress. Leaders who take action despite uncertainty build resilience, foster innovation, and gain experience. Hesitating to act can result in stagnation and limit your ability to seize opportunities as they arise.

What to Reflect On:

- Do you often delay decisions because you're unsure of the outcome?

- How comfortable are you with taking calculated risks, even when the path is unclear?
- Are you willing to trust your instincts and make decisions without having all the answers?
- How could embracing uncertainty and taking action lead to faster growth and success?

Answering YES indicates that hesitation in uncertainty may hold you back, and acting decisively could unlock new growth opportunities.

Answering NO suggests that you are willing to take action despite uncertainty, positioning yourself for continuous progress and success.

SEQ 23: You need to invest in building strong relationships.

Why It Matters:

Strong relationships are the backbone of personal and professional success. Building meaningful connections fosters trust, collaboration, and support, all essential in leadership and life. When you invest time cultivating relationships, you create networks of people who can offer advice, share opportunities, and help you grow. Leaders who prioritise relationships thrive in teams and communities, making their path to success smoother and more fulfilling.

What to Reflect On:

- Do you prioritize building strong relationships with those around you?
- How often do you make an effort to connect with others on a deeper level, beyond surface interactions?
- Are you actively nurturing your existing relationships to ensure they remain strong and mutually beneficial?
- How could investing more in relationship-building enhance your leadership, collaboration, and personal growth?

Answering YES Indicates that you may need to emphasise building strong relationships to strengthen your leadership and opportunities.

Answering NO suggests that you already focus on cultivating meaningful connections and positioning yourself for long-term success through strong networks and relationships.

SEQ 24: You often ignore red flags.

Why It Matters:

Ignoring red flags can lead to significant problems in personal relationships, business decisions, or leadership challenges. Red flags serve as early warning signs that something requires attention, and when you dismiss them, you risk letting minor issues escalate into major obstacles. Leaders who acknowledge and address red flags early can prevent future setbacks, maintain trust, and keep their teams or projects on track.

What to Reflect On:

- Do you often overlook signs of potential issues in relationships, work, or projects?
- How comfortable are you with confronting problems or uncomfortable truths when they arise?
- Are you willing to investigate red flags further, even if it means making tough decisions?
- How could addressing red flags sooner help you avoid more significant challenges and maintain steady progress?

Answering YES indicates that ignoring red flags might be causing avoidable problems, and addressing them sooner could lead to smoother paths and greater success.

Answering NO suggests that you are proactive in recognizing and dealing with issues, positioning yourself for effective leadership and problem-solving.

SEQ 25: You keep maintaining a negative mindset.

Why It Matters:

A negative mindset can limit your potential, weaken your motivation, and prevent you from seeing opportunities for growth and success. Your mindset shapes how you respond to challenges and influences your overall well-being. Leaders who cultivate a positive, solution-focused mindset are better equipped to overcome obstacles, inspire others, and pave the way for success. Shifting from negativity to optimism allows you to approach life and leadership with greater resilience and clarity.

What to Reflect On:

- Do you often focus on the negative aspects of situations rather than potential solutions or opportunities?
- How frequently does a negative mindset affect your decisions, actions, or interactions with others?
- Are you willing to actively work on reframing challenges and setbacks in a more positive, constructive light?
- How could adopting a more positive mindset enhance your leadership, problem-solving, and overall success?

Answering YES Indicates that a negative mindset may be holding you back, and adopting a more positive approach could unlock more significant growth and opportunities.

Answering NO suggests that you maintain a constructive mindset while positioning yourself for greater resilience, motivation, and success.

SEQ 26: You keep quitting too early.

Why It Matters:

Quitting too early can prevent you from realizing your full potential and achieving your long-term goals. Success often requires persistence, even in the face of challenges or slow progress. Leaders who push through setbacks and stay committed to their vision are likely to experience breakthroughs and lasting success. Quitting prematurely can leave untapped opportunities on the table, while resilience and perseverance often lead to the results you're aiming for.

What to Reflect On:

- Do you tend to give up on goals or projects when progress feels slow or difficult?
- How often do you reassess your commitment when facing obstacles instead of pushing through them?
- Are you willing to stay the course, even when success seems far away or uncertain?
- How could developing more persistence help you achieve greater results and unlock new growth opportunities?

Answering YES Indicates that quitting too soon may hinder your success, and pushing through challenges could lead to greater rewards and long-term achievement.

Answering NO suggests that you are committed to staying the course, which positions you for continuous growth and eventual success, even when the journey is tough.

SEQ 27: You frequently neglect empathy.

Why It Matters:

Empathy is a crucial leadership skill that builds trust, strengthens relationships, and fosters collaboration. Neglecting empathy can lead to misunderstandings, conflict, and a lack of connection. Leaders prioritising empathy create environments where people feel heard, valued, and supported. Empathy allows you to understand the perspectives and emotions of others better, improving communication and teamwork and ultimately leading to more effective leadership and personal success.

What to Reflect On:

- Do you explore to understand the feelings and perspectives of those around you?
- How often do you listen deeply to others, showing genuine concern for their emotions and challenges?
- Are you willing to put yourself in someone else's shoes, even when difficult or uncomfortable?
- How could practising more empathy improve your relationships, leadership effectiveness, and overall impact?

Answering YES Indicates that neglecting empathy may hinder your ability to connect with others and lead effectively, and increasing empathy could enhance your leadership.

Answering NO suggests that you prioritise empathy, positioning yourself to build stronger, more trusting relationships, and achieving greater success through compassion and understanding.

9.

27 Ways to Success, Greatness, Happiness and Richness

1. Embrace Failure as a Teacher
2. Success is a Marathon, not a Sprint
3. Passion Alone Isn't Enough—Pair It with Strategy
4. Create Your Own Luck with Preparation
5. Money is a Tool, Not the Goal
6. Innovation Wins Over Tradition
7. Build with Discipline, Thrive with Consistency
8. Take Calculated Risks for Maximum Growth
9. Success Requires Both Hard and Smart Work
10. Perfection is the Enemy of Progress
11. Combine Emotional Intelligence with Rational Thinking

12. Confidence and Humility Go Hand in Hand
13. Adaptability is Your Advantage
14. Think Long-Term, Act Short-Term
15. Success is Collective, Not Solo
16. Master Decision-Making
17. Balance Work and Life for Richness
18. Resilience is Your Strength
19. Manage Stress Effectively
20. Leverage Technology for a Digital Edge
21. Build Strong Networks, But Depend on Yourself
22. Keep Learning, Stay Curious
23. Let Your Purpose Drive Your Success
24. You, Not Society, Define Success
25. Growth Alone Does Not Measure Success
26. Learn to Delegate and Empower Others
27. True Richness Comes from Gratitude

Summary

21 Secrets to Success, Greatness, Happiness, and Richness is more than just a book—it's a transformative journey that redefines what it means to achieve success, greatness, happiness, and richness. This book guides readers in breaking free from conventional narratives in a world clouded by misconceptions and unrealistic expectations. Demystifying common myths and providing practical insights empower readers to create a personal definition of success that aligns with their values and goals.

The book dives deep into **21 myths** about success, greatness, happiness, and richness—misconceptions that often lead people to believe success comes easily or that personal fulfilment requires sacrificing everything else. Each myth is dissected to reveal the truth underneath, helping you gain clarity on what truly matters. This clarity is paired with actionable strategies, allowing you to forge a path toward a more balanced and meaningful version of success.

To help you internalize and act upon these insights, **21 Success Possibilities (SPs)** are introduced, providing a framework for personal growth and self-reflection. These quadrants serve as a diagnostic tool to evaluate where you currently stand in different areas of life. Understanding your position helps you identify your strengths and weaknesses, guiding you toward intentional improvement and sustainable achievement.

Accompanying these SPs are **Success Evaluation Questions (SEQs)** that invite deep self-reflection and challenge you to examine your habits, mindset, and behaviours. These questions cover vital areas such as goal setting, resilience, adaptability, and personal fulfilment, encouraging growth by aligning your actions with your deeper values. By regularly revisiting these questions, you can better understand your personal and professional growth journey.

Key Takeaways:

1. **Redefine Success**: Success, greatness, happiness, and richness are personal journeys shaped by your unique values and aspirations.

2. **Debunk the Myths**: Break free from limiting beliefs and discover the truths that will empower you to create a more fulfilling life.

3. **Reflect and Grow**: Use the Success Possibilities and Evaluation Questions to evaluate your current path and identify areas for personal development.

4. **Commit to Lifelong Improvement**: Continuous learning, self-reflection, and adaptability are vital to lasting success.

Concrete/Clear Call to Action (CCTA):

1. As you finish **21 Secrets to Success, Greatness, Happiness, and Richness**, don't let the insights you've gained fade away.
2. Take immediate action by applying what you've learned.
3. Revisit the Success Evaluation Questions regularly, assess where you fall within the Quadrants of Possibilities, and challenge any myths lingering in your mind.

Success, greatness, happiness, and richness aren't destinations; they are processes of continuous growth and learning. Stay committed to your journey, align with your core values, and remain adaptable in the face of change. Remember, you hold the power to define your path.

Are you ready to take control of your life's narrative? Start by setting a clear, achievable goal today. Use the principles and tools provided in this book to create a personalized roadmap for your future. Share your progress, seek out new opportunities, and uplift others. Your journey has the potential to inspire greatness in those around you, so don't hold back.

Act now—your true success awaits.

Farookh Sensei

www.ingramcontent.com/pod-product-compliance
Ingram Content Group UK Ltd.
Pitfield, Milton Keynes, MK11 3LW, UK
UKHW040006200726
13854UKWH00001B/65

9 798896 108849